PRACTICE GREATNESS

PRACTICE
GREATNESS

ESCAPE SMALL THINKING, LISTEN LIKE A MASTER, AND LEAD WITH YOUR BEST

AMIEL HANDELSMAN

JZ LEADERSHIP PRESS

Published by JZ Leadership Press, Portland, OR

Amiel Handelsman, 1970-
Portland, OR
amiel@amielhandelsman.com
amielhandelsman.com

ISBN 978-0-9895895-2-9
First Edition

Cover by Sarah Heckles

Printed in the United States of America

To Ben Handelsman

CONTENTS

1 IN 10,000 CHANCE

"THAT'S IMPOSSIBLE! THE doctor said we had a one in ten thousand chance."

It was just past 10 a.m. in Portland, and I was standing in the bathroom next to my wife. She had just pulled me out of a post-brunch conversation I was having in our living room with two friends. With a radiant smile on her face, she held up a small test strip showing a "plus" sign.

"Look, Amiel," she replied. "It's right there. This means we're pregnant."

"Julie, that line looks faint. It can't be right. One in ten thousand chance. Do you really think we are that one?"

She smiled.

I realized then that I wasn't going to win this argument even though I was obviously right. And she *was* glowing. What business did I have spoiling such an uplifting moment, however misconstrued? So I took a deep breath, said, "Well, let's hope so," gave her a kiss, and returned to our friends.

Eight months later, our son, Jacob, was born.

That was the first inspiration for writing a book about opening your mind and heart to the possibility of life's greatness.

SNEAK PREVIEW

THIS BOOK IS a how-to guide with an edge. The edge arises from three beefs I have with many popular leadership books:

1. They claim to show you how to become a better leader, but don't provide actionable recommendations. *Actionable* means that it's physical; you can capture it on videotape. Giving leaders actual phrases to incorporate into questions is actionable. Instructing them to ask better questions is not. This book provides phrases.

2. They emphasize leaders' outer behaviors and ignore their thoughts, feelings, and worldviews. This book provides both outer and inner practices of great leadership.

3. They treat all leaders the same. Ever read a book instructing you to be "bolder?" I'm all for boldness, but for many leaders this isn't the most important quality to cultivate. In fact, I've worked with leaders who are bold to a fault. They need to learn to pause

and consider the impact of their decisions before acting. This book assumes that different leaders have different needs.

This book is organized to provide answers to three questions:

1. Why don't organizations produce great leadership today?

2. What are the outer and inner practices of great leadership?

3. How can you successfully take on these practices, from who you are now, within the organization where you work?

Part One answers the *why* question. Parts Two and Three answer the *what* question. Part Four answers the *how* question. Part Five looks at these issues from an organizational perspective. By the time you're finished, you may be asking the *who* question: if you step fully into practicing greatness and transform how you speak, listen, and think, who could you become?

Part One begins with an account of my own experience in the leadership development field: the questions I grappled with, the lessons I learned, and how these transformed my work. Then, we review several pivotal research studies and find that what works best in leadership development is very different from what is popular today. For example, it turns out that on-the-job learning produces better results than even the best formal training. And organizations get a better return on investment when their top executives personally "own" leadership development and when managers at every level develop the managers who report to them.

Just when you start feeling hungry to put these insights into action, I add another layer of frosting to the cake. We examine what the leadership development field can learn from talent hotbeds in sports, music, and the theatrical arts. The phrase *deliberate practice* becomes central to our discussion. Then we take a candid look at three obstacles to developing great leadership. At this point, you realize that this book is for real people working in an imperfect world. I then outline fifteen practices of great leadership and describe where they came from. Hint: it's about taking the best and jettisoning the rest. Finally, I ask "To what end?" and "Where will you focus?"

At this point, if you're still excited by the promise of great leadership, you'll find in Parts Two and Three a specific set of practices for becoming this kind of leader—not just when it's convenient, but all of the time.

Part Two contains eight practices that are visible to others, so I call them "outer" practices:

- I describe how trying to find a girlfriend taught me about *conversations for possibility*, and how specifically to design and hold these kinds of conversations in your organization. (Chapter 8)

- I invite you to pay close attention to the hundreds of "micro-interactions" you have each day. You will see why *turning toward* other people in these micro-interactions builds trust, why turning away from and turning against others doesn't, and how to turn toward others more consistently. (Chapter 9)

- If all of this turning doesn't leave you too dizzy—or if it does and you start complaining about it—you'll enjoy the next challenge: taking your everyday complaints seriously. Not by believing them, but by finding within them the signs of what matters most to you. *Flipping these complaints* and publicly declaring the commitments you discover within them has great potential to positively affect the mood of your team and organization. This flip isn't something you learned in school, so I provide a five-step approach to carrying it out. (Chapter 10)

- After providing an amusing recipe for mediocre arguing, I offer five suggestions for how to *argue better*. For example, by distinguishing assessments from factual assertions and asking others to ground their assessments; in short: by not being an arrogant know-it-all. (Chapter 11)

- I describe why *storytelling* is a powerful leadership tool and suggest resources for developing your competence at this. (Chapter 12)

- After challenging popular notions about listening, I reveal the secrets of *listening like a master*. For example, what specifically gets in the way of your listening well to others? (Chapter 13)

- I describe why *asking* "dumb" *questions* is smart and offer specific "power phrases" you can use to make your dumb questions even dumber. This section alone is worth the price of the book, and that's before we get into the mood and intention behind your questions. Words aren't everything! (Chapter 14)

- Part Two concludes with pointers on *making peace with your enemies*. I propose a five-point scale for assessing the quality of your relationships and ask you to determine which are truly pivotal to your success. Then I provide suggestions for mending pivotal relationships that are currently broken. (Chapter 15)

Part Three introduces seven "inner" practices of great leadership. These practices are all real, tangible things you can do that others may or may not see, depending upon where you do them:

- I describe what Kirk Gibson can teach us about *visualizing* big possibilities and how you can do this yourself. Hint: start with, "Wouldn't it be great if____?" (Chapter 16)

- Stories about Intel and Honda remind us that many of the best strategies are not deliberate but emergent. Strategies emerge when you learn how to recognize patterns of behavior from the past, such as market shifts and how your middle managers respond to them. This skill of *seeing patterns* will also allow you to spot hidden strengths in your team. (Chapter 17)

- I introduce nine distinctive *"Achilles' Heels."* One is likely a source of vulnerability for you that can be healed. (Chapter 18)

- Then I take this a step further by challenging you to *"call B.S." on yourself*—and, yes, I even spell out what those initials stand for. Parental advisory encouraged. (Chapter 19)

- I acknowledge how difficult it is to take on new practices when life is already full. This leads to tips on how to create a trusted system for *managing commitments*: all the projects, activities, and actions that matter to you. And the stuff that doesn't matter? Enter "Dumpster Days" at stage left. (Chapter 20)

- I focus on one topic that is so important it is rarely mentioned in any leadership book: how to *manage your physical energy* to meet the extraordinary demands of being a manager. I share the best lessons my clients have used in the areas of sleeping, exercise, nutrition, and renewal. (Chapter 21)

- With your attention now focused on your body, I invite you to consider your body *posture*—what it is, and the enormous impact it has on your mood and your openness to possibility. (Chapter 22)

Part Four is about how to *practice* great leadership. It describes what we can learn from competitive athletes, elite musicians, and top theatrical artists. We explore how to translate these insights into tangible methods of practice in your organization:

- I describe the attributes of *deliberate practice* and four ways to do this *directly*: the music approach, the chess approach, the sports conditioning approach, and the sports simulation approach. Plus I give you specific secrets from talent hotbeds. You'll realize that you already know everything you need to know about how to practice. What's left to do is employ this knowledge in a new context. (Chapter 23)

- I introduce a four-step *on-the-job practice cycle*. I discuss how to *prepare* your mind and body before you *act*, give you specific questions you can use to *reflect* afterwards, and discuss the attributes of high-quality *feedback* and how you can ensure that you are receiving it. (Chapter 24)

- I ask you to consider what *challenging experiences* will help you grow and how to get these experiences in either your current job or a new job. (Chapter 25)

Part Five is written for people responsible for improving leadership development across an organization: HR leaders, learning and development managers, and talent-minded executives. The central question we explore is how to produce the greatest return for your leadership development dollar:

- I introduce the concept of Return on Improved Performance and suggest ways to apply this to leadership development. I discuss how you can decide which leaders to develop, how much to invest in each leader, and which skills will produce the largest overall improved performance. (Chapter 26)

- I offer specific tips for designing the following activities in a way that maximizes learning and skill-building: top talent selection, succession planning, executive coaching, development plans, cohort learning, action learning, formal training, and strategy execution. (Chapter 27)

The book concludes with the experiences of three people who have made the leap from practicing great leadership to integrating it into their *way of being*.

Practice Greatness includes stories from my own experience to remind you—and me—that we are all learning about this topic together.

Amiel Handelsman
amiel@amielhandelsman.com
Portland, Oregon
February 15, 2014

PRACTICE GREATNESS

A Better Way to Develop Leadership

Chapter 1
Why Focus on Greatness?

A YEAR AFTER the birth of my son, Jacob, the second inspiration for this book came in a conference room of a large corporation. Steve (a pseudonym) and I were sitting across the table from each other. This was our first meeting, and he had an important question for me.

"Look," he said. "I've been working here for 15 years, and I've been to a lot of leadership classes. The one I went to last month was far and away the best, particularly the part about possibility thinking. That's not how we usually do things here, so it had a big impact on me—almost hard to describe. When I walked out, I felt like something had changed in me. But then I got back into the job here…" He paused and gulped. "Well, let's just say it's been hard to maintain that same excitement. My days are very full. There's a lot of pressure. So… how do you suggest I keep it going?"

"What in particular would you like to keep going?" I asked.

"I need to focus on what's possible rather than what's wrong. Listening to people rather than just arguing with them. This could make a big difference in my group, and I have to lead the way. Can you help me?"

"Yes, I can help you," I replied.

And that is what I proceeded to do—not only with Steve, but with fifteen other highly successful managers in his company. All of them had taken the same seminar and experienced a powerful "aha" moment unlike any they had experienced before. And all of them were finding it difficult to extend that moment into an ongoing lived reality. What they really wanted was confirmation from their own experience that what they saw in that seminar—a new way of leading, indeed a new way of living—was real. Not an error or aberration, but something that could produce tangible results in a company of hard-nosed people.

It was almost as though these managers had been shown a test strip with a plus sign that indicated "possible" rather than "pregnant." They wanted to believe that this plus sign was accurate because it would mean a new way of experiencing life. However, they had been around the block long enough to hold this faith lightly, and they were unclear how to start.

In reality, their leadership journey had already started… and then been sidetracked. My job as their coach was not only to help them get back on track, but also to reframe what the journey was about and what it would take to complete it.

This journey is complex, and my understanding of it has evolved over time. Initially, to honor the specific challenges these sixteen leaders faced, I called it the journey from fear to possibility. *Fear* describes not these managers as individuals but a key piece of the organizational culture in which they learned to manage. This quality shows up in several ways: conversations in which people critique what's wrong with ideas rather than explore what's right, fear-based control systems that waste time and drain human energy, and performance management approaches that foster unhealthy competition at the expense of collaboration. The journey from fear to possibility presents two main challenges:

- How do you lead people to explore new possibilities and trust each other when the culture has historically discouraged these things?
- Once you've developed a new approach to leadership, how do you use it to transform this very culture?

These challenges—and the larger journey from fear to possibility—are not unique to the sixteen managers at this company. In my twenty years developing leaders, I've seen them show up in countless places, from Fortune 100 companies to professional service firms to large health care systems to government agencies to relatively small not-for-profit organizations. Not every organization has a fear-based culture, but many do, and every one that does is filled with managers looking for a better way to lead.

That's why I originally conceived this book as a guide for managers working in fear-based cultures.

And then something surprising happened.

When I sent out an earlier version of the book to clients and colleagues around the world, the response was overwhelmingly positive, but in a way I had not expected. People loved the book, but thought it applied to a much broader audience. Not just people working in fear-based cultures, but leaders everywhere committed to elevating their game.

This feedback caused me to take a hard look at the contents of the book. Was it relevant only to fear-based organizations, or did it indeed apply more widely? I reviewed the leadership practices that comprised the heart of the book. As I considered where they came from and the organizations in which they had proved useful, the answer was clear: these practices are about much more than shifting from fear to possibility. They describe a second journey, one that is relevant to anyone deliberately trying to lead organizations better.

This is the journey to greatness.

When you see the word *greatness*, particularly in the context of leadership or organizations, what does it bring up in your mind? Many people associate greatness with leaders who died decades ago or, in the case of Nelson Mandela, passed away recently but made their marks in what now feels like a different era. Others believe that greatness is born—and only in rare individuals. Indeed, they think it is so rare that if we actually tested the DNA of great leaders, we would discover that they are a different species. (Homo greatiens?) Altogether, most of us grudgingly accept the notion of great leadership but then think: *not this year, and certainly not in my organization.*

I, for one, have long shied away from using the word *great* to describe anything associated with me. Growing up in Ann Arbor, Michigan, I learned that football players could be great, bands could be great, and teachers could be great. But people running organizations, like mayors, fire chiefs, bank CEOs, and grocery store owners, were either mediocre, OK, or good. Greatness was not on the radar. Later, in two decades as a change consultant and executive coach, I never (until recently) told anyone they could become great by following my guidance. It seemed like too big a promise to make.

Yet here's the thing. When I reflect upon the best leaders I've coached, observed, met, or heard about, it becomes clear that greatness is not about emulating someone else. If it were, we would all be guaranteed to fail. Instead, greatness is about realizing our own full potential—being the best version of ourselves—in a domain of life (such as work, parenting, partnering, athletics, or art) that matters to us. Great *leadership* is about doing this for the sake of a purpose larger than ourselves. To summarize:

Greatness = realizing our full potential in a particular domain of life

Great Leadership = realizing our full potential for the sake of a larger purpose

Once we reframe greatness and great leadership in this way, our assessment of these concepts can change: *Maybe* (you whisper to yourself) *greatness is possible today. Perhaps it's even possible in my organization.*

There is another reason I've come to accept greatness as a suitable aspiration. This one was in front of me for years, but I never noticed it. The leaders I coach—and people everywhere trying to improve their effectiveness within organizations—cannot get better from a series of "aha" moments. Nor can they improve by wishing things would improve, creating a written development plan, or even hiring an executive coach. Instead, getting better at leading requires the same ingredient as getting better at soccer or the violin: deliberate practice. This means repeating a skill over and over again for the explicit purpose of learning and getting continuous feedback from a skilled coach or teacher. Although this can largely be done on the job, it takes focus, discipline, and yes, hard work.

This is where greatness enters the picture. Research on high performing athletes and musicians shows that people are far more likely to do the hard work of deliberate practice if they can imagine themselves performing at the highest level of their sport, profession, or trade—and *want* to do what it will take to get there. Daniel Coyle, author of *The Talent Code*, suggests that this motivating force often appears in a single moment. For example, he points out that South Korea had no history of success in women's golf until May 18, 1998. That was the day Se Ri Pak won the McDonald's LPGA Championship. A nation of women instantly got inspired to compete—and practice. A decade later, South Korea's female golfers were winning one third of all tour events.

Pak's victory is an example of what Coyle calls "ignition." It's the moment when ordinary people decide to dedicate themselves to extraordinary skill development. Coyle states that:

Ignition is a hot, mysterious burst, an awakening…[that] works through lightning flashes of image and emotion, evolution-built neural programs that tap into the mind's vast reserves of energy and attention. [It's about] the moments that lead us to say *that is who I want to be.*

So we find ourselves in an interesting situation. If you want to get better at leading, you need to deliberately practice. However, you will only invest the energy to practice if you imagine yourself performing at a much higher level than you are now. Going from mediocre to OK or from OK to good won't suffice. The ignition you need to practice is a "lightning flash" image of being the very best version of yourself.

Luckily, we already have a term for this: greatness.

To summarize:

Great Leadership = Ignition + Deliberate Practice

Here we come to a wonderful irony. It's actually easier to get better at leading if you shoot for greatness than if you just try to do a bit better. If your goal is simply to get a promotion, feel a bit less stressed, or get your boss off your back, you're unlikely to be ignited to practice the relevant skills. However, if your goal is to do something extraordinary by being the best version of yourself, you will have the ignition to practice. As a result, you'll not only raise your odds of getting a promotion (or reducing stress or pleasing your boss), but you're also more likely to make the impact you intend to make in your life.

You will be practicing greatness.

CHAPTER 2
DEVELOPING LEADERSHIP—
WHAT WORKS

"IF THERE IS indeed a right stuff for executives, it may be this extraordinary tenacity at extracting something worthwhile from their experience and in seeking experiences rich in opportunities for growth."

 —Morgan McCall, Michael Lombardo, and Ann Morrison, *The Lessons of Experience: How Successful Executives Develop On The Job*

When I entered the executive development field in the mid 1990s, the tools and techniques that are now dominant were just starting to blossom. Seminars offered by business schools and training companies introduced leaders to new ways of conceptualizing their work (e.g. situational leadership, the stages of team development, and visioning) and used assessment instruments (e.g. Myers-Briggs, FIRO-B, SYMLOG, and the Thomas-Kilmann Conflict Mode Instrument) to expose their blind spots. The premise was that if we gave people new cognitive models of what constitutes excellence and large amounts of data about how they were perceived by coworkers, they would be both motivated to change and know how to change. Often, these workshops contained simulations, games, and role plays, but the bulk of the time was devoted to cognitive learning and review of feedback data.

The company where I worked offered a particularly rigorous program to the country's leading health care executives. During a five-day seminar at a premier executive education center, participants received feedback from eight separate assessment instruments. Our trainers patiently walked people through the data, explained the theories behind it, and helped them make sense of it in the context of their jobs. These trainers were both wise and compassionate, both firm and loving—the kinds of people who immediately put you at ease. In this safe, reflective environment, it was common for leaders to finish the week inspired by the insights they had received and committed to making changes in their lives. But, we knew that good intentions were not enough. To truly change, they needed to follow through "on Monday morning." So, in order to ensure that participants sustained their learning, we asked them to commit to an action plan before they got on the shuttle to the airport to head home.

I felt proud to be connected with this program. Not only were we serving top executives at some of the country's most prestigious health care institutions, but we were engaging them in a noble pursuit: improving the way they led their organizations. And we were doing it using the latest and most scientific approaches to leadership development. To create this program, we took a highly regarded three-day course offered by the Center for Creative Leadership, added two days, and doubled the number of instruments. Since our trainers understood experiential learning better than most, we also asked participants to give each other live feedback about behaviors they had observed during the program. At the end of the week, each participant spent two hours with a coach integrating all they had learned. As I sometimes joked to friends, it was the Mercedes Benz of executive development courses.

Only years later did I realize what was missing from this program and many others like it. We gave people data-driven insights and wonderful models, but we neglected to address an important question: what does it take to integrate these insights into your everyday life so that they inform how you speak, listen, and interact with others? Indeed, how can you embed "aha" moments into your physiology so that your body carries them as it moves through life? Yes, we asked participants to create action plans. But, in retrospect, I think that even our senior trainers—some of the best in the country—knew in their guts that actions plans are inadequate methods of creating embodied learning. Like strategic plans, they look good on paper but often end up gathering dust in filing cabinets or on bookshelves.

For several years, I wrestled with this question: after leaders have finished a powerful training program, how do we help them integrate what they learned into their everyday work lives? One option was to make follow up calls several months later. A second option, since this was the mid-1990s during the rise of the Internet, was to send them a weekly email reminding them to pay attention to what matters most. Or we could invite them back for another workshop and hope that they had the interest and budget for it.

During the period these questions were alive for me, I discovered the field of executive coaching. I learned that some organizations hired people to work one-on-one with their leaders on an ongoing basis, not just during training programs. I read more about this field, contacted several local coaches, and soon began coaching students in a graduate program in sustainable business, as well as a few business managers. I didn't have a coherent coaching methodology or any training in coaching, so I relied on my favorite models from leadership training like William Bridge's three stages of transition (endings, neutral zone, and new beginnings).

11

My clients appreciated my good questions and deep listening but generally lost interest after a handful of sessions. One reason for this was that I wasn't charging them: they didn't have any skin in the game. A second was that my bag of tricks wasn't big enough to encompass my clients' concerns. Bridges's transitions framework was great, but it wasn't the best match for many people's situations. The real reason, though, was that I still didn't have an answer to the question: how do you help people integrate insights into their everyday lives?

Fortunately, before subjecting too many people to my half-baked coaching, I discovered an approach—and a community—that changed my life. In New Hampshire, at a meeting of the Society for Organizational Learning, I met a consultant named Andrea Dyer. She worked as a coach to many of the top executives at a Fortune 100 company and appeared to be earning a good living doing so. I learned that rather than simply transferring concepts and methods from her consulting and leadership development work as I had done, she prepared for such high level coaching work by being enrolled in a formal coach training program with a company called New Ventures West.

Wow, I thought to myself. *She coaches Fortune 100 executives. I coach mostly graduate students. If she needs training in coaching, then I really need it!*

Less than a year later, I was enrolled in New Ventures West's professional coaching course. This intensive year-long program taught me three major things. First, it convinced me that trying to apply a few simple leadership models to a wide variety of human beings wasn't going to cut it. My clients needed me to come to them with a broader, richer, and more rigorous foundation. Second, it taught me a structured methodology for coaching people, one that contained specific stages yet enough flexibility to flow with people's experience. Finally and most importantly, I found an answer to the riddle that I'd been wrestling with for years: how do you help people integrate insights into their everyday lives? You encourage them to practice new skills and qualities, and you invite them to actively reflect on their own experiences. Practice and reflection. Or, to be precise, practice and self-observation, which is the act of non-judgmentally reflecting on your experience while you are in the midst of that experience. It is reflection-in-action.

During this program, I learned both practice and self-observation by doing them myself. I took an Aikido class to learn how to blend with others' power rather than fight them or withdraw. To develop my courage, I kept a journal of brave actions I had taken that day. My self-observation consisted of watching myself throughout the day and noticing when I felt connected with others and when I felt disconnected. After several months of doing these exercises with the support of my classmates and the faculty, I started to practice the methodology with clients. Early in my relationship with them, I helped them reframe whatever situation they were facing (a big new job, a possible geographic move, a career transition) by making a distinction that helped them see their situation and themselves in new ways. Then I designed practices and self-observation exercises for them. Remarkably, although I was just a beginner at it, the approach (known as Integral Coaching) worked. People practiced. They observed themselves in action—or at least reflected afterwards. As a result, they got better at their work and more skillful in their lives.

After completing the year-long program, I spent some time reflecting on how radically this approach to developing people differed from formal leadership training. Rather than starting with conceptual models of what it means to be a good leader or happy person, we started with the concerns and commitments of the human beings in front of us. And rather than doing this in a training setting, we did it while people were in the middle of their experiences.

The old starting point: Conceptual models

The new starting point: The concerns and commitments of the people in front of you

The old equation: Leadership Development = Formal Training + ?

The new equation: Leadership Development = Powerful Insights + Practice + Self-Observation

Ironically, it took a formal training program (albeit a highly unconventional one) to disabuse me of the notion that leadership development starts with formal training. And it required a year-long immersion in developing myself and others to realize that my own curriculum in leadership development and human development (what I needed to learn) had only just begun. New Ventures West had crafted the outline and a great starting point. My job was to fill in the details.

In subsequent years, as I grew my coaching practice and worked with more senior executives at larger organizations, I remained dedicated to improving my craft. Each engagement was an opportunity to try out new approaches and see what worked. Each conversation challenged me to remain fully present, rather than getting distracted by competing thoughts or concerns. During this time, I read widely, not only about leadership, but also about happiness, high performance, adult learning, developmental psychology, somatics (the study of the human body and how it shapes what's possible in life), and language (how we create relationships, possibilities, and action through speaking and listening). Whenever possible, I reached out to colleagues to compare notes on our respective work and what we were reading.

Over time, these experiences crystallized into a discovery and an obsession. The discovery was that nearly everything that seemed important in leadership and in life—excellence, high performance, happiness, and resilience—grew through long-term dedicated practice. The obsession was two-fold. First, I wanted to help people find one or two truly pivotal practices, those with the greatest chance of improving their leadership and life for the better. Second, I wanted to help them embed these practices into very full lives.

This obsession—and a consulting engagement with a large company exploring how to better develop its top talent—led me to an intensive research project centered on these questions:

- What are the most effective ways for organizations to improve the quality of their leadership at every level?
- What are most organizations doing instead? Why aren't they doing what works?
- What would it look like—and what sacred cows would need to be slain—to build leadership development around what works rather than what is popular?

As I examined three decades of research, what emerged was a clear picture of how to successfully develop leadership. As we shall see, it is very different from what most organizations are doing. This successful strategy includes:

1. Managers who can use on-the-job experience to learn the pivotal lessons they need to guide their organizations into the future.

2. Top executives who are personally accountable for developing leadership.

3. Managers at every level who are actively and skillfully involved in developing their direct reports.

HOW CAN MANAGERS LEARN PIVOTAL LESSONS THROUGH ON-THE-JOB EXPERIENCE?

Over thirty years ago, the Center for Creative Leadership (CCL) conducted one of the first serious studies of outstanding leadership. In extensive interviews with successful executives, they asked these individuals what experiences had shaped them the most. You may not be surprised to hear that the vast preponderance of learning happened through on-the-job experience, not formal training. To be specific, 48 percent came from assignments, 18 percent from people, 17 percent from hardships, and 11 percent from other sources. Merely 6 percent of learning came from courses, and learning occurred *only* if the subject matter matched what they were learning on the job. (Later studies refined this into the 70/20/10 rule: 70 percent experience, 20 percent people, and 10 percent formal training.[1]) As the researchers wrote in their 1988 book *The Lessons of Experience*:

> The challenge lies in making use of on-the-job experiences. This means finding better ways to identify developmentally significant jobs, to move the right people to them...and to help talented people learn from them. How well these things are done is far more important than how formal or elegant the procedures are.

A 2005 report by the Corporate Leadership Council reached nearly identical conclusions. Of more than 300 developmental strategies, only 80 moved potential in a meaningful way. The three clusters that mattered were "structuring challenges within job experiences that unlock learning, leveraging relationships, and ensuring credible organizational commitment."[2] Similarly, Robert Eichinger, a longtime leadership expert, noted that the only development approaches that "by themselves move a skill"[3] are full-time jobs and part-time assignments like task forces and special projects. Finally, Lominger, one of the big names in the leadership development space, found that "leaders with higher scores on the Learning Agility instrument perform better once promoted."[4]

To summarize, the research tells us that if you want to develop leaders, do the following:

1. Identify challenging experiences that unlock key lessons.

2. Give these experiences to people who are most likely to learn from them.

3. Provide these individuals with the necessary organizational support to accelerate their learning.

This formula makes sense, doesn't it? I bet it matches what you've witnessed in your own life. Consider the capabilities you have developed as a leader. Did you learn them from a training course or from on-the-job experience?

The notion of learning from experience is familiar. However, the CCL researchers discovered something else that may come as news to you: not all experiences are equally useful. There is a distinct set of challenging experiences that teach leadership lessons far better than others. The original CCL study named 17 such experiences.[5] An updated study in the past decade, which looked at African American and women leaders (as compared to the original study of white men), added six more, for a total of 23 experiences.[6] For example, here are five of the challenging experiences that stand out to me because many leaders I coach are in the midst of them:

- Starting from scratch
- Turnarounds
- Increased scope
- Line-to-staff switch
- Special bosses (very good or very bad)

According to CCL researchers, these five experiences and the rest on their list tend to produce more and better learning for the leaders who have them (assuming, again, that these leaders are adept at learning from experience).

As you look at the list, you may be thinking, *Well, of course!*

But is this how your organization is developing its leaders? When managers and HR staff get together to discuss this topic, does the conversation focus on the pivotal experiences that will teach leaders what they need to learn to chart your organization's path over the next five years? Do they talk about which rising stars will make the most of these experiences and thereby provide the greatest return on investment? Or does the conversation revolve around competencies and training?

Furthermore, when it's time to create a development plan for yourself, do your manager and HR Business Partner help you identify the lessons you can learn from your current job and future roles—and how to unlock the most learning? Or are you asked to make sense of a 360 instrument that contains a large list of competencies that sound rigorously scientific yet contain words that you and your peers rarely use and don't know how to put into action? Does the action plan portion of your development plan list task forces and special assignments, or does it consist mostly of training courses and books?

I have a hunch about the answer to these questions.

Now, let's talk about a pivotal decision that managers control and that holds enormous leverage for developing leaders: who to hire. When senior managers in your organization hire people, do they ask themselves, which up-and-coming leaders can learn the most from this experience so they'll be ready for bigger roles? Or do they simply hire the most qualified person, someone who may or may not learn the lessons the experience teaches and therefore may or may not be propelled to future success at more senior levels? There is an enormous difference between these two sets of criteria. (By the way, I'm not advocating for hiring solely based on who learns best. Good hiring managers consider both performance *and* learning. They also assess the risk and cost of failure of hiring somebody who is not 100 percent ready for the role.)

Finally, a few words about succession planning. It's been a hot topic in many companies for the past 10–15 years, driven by rapid CEO turnover, the realization that most boards govern poorly, and increased public attention to the "war for talent." More recently, the public sector has placed greater emphasis on succession planning, largely because of the pending retirement of the massive Baby Boomer generation. Does your organization have a team or task force focused on how to source and develop its future senior executives? If so, what criteria is it using to identify these people? Is it making decisions based solely on past performance? Or is it also considering a person's capacity to learn (which is sometimes called learning agility)?

I recently asked this question to people guiding talent development strategies at two different Fortune 500 corporations. Both told me that their companies used two criteria: performance and potential. The tool they employ is known as the 9 Box Performance-Potential Matrix, or 9 Box for short. (Each person is assessed as low, medium, or high on past performance and low, medium, or high on potential). When I asked them how their companies assessed people's potential, their responses were remarkably similar: "Not very rigorously, and mostly based on what folks have done before." In other words, the companies assessed potential based upon past performance. These organizations weren't actually using two criteria to pick successors. They were using one. And the capacity to learn from experience wasn't part of the decision.

If your organization focuses on competencies rather than learning and thinks that leaders develop through training rather than on-the-job experience, it is not alone. The vast majority of large corporations, government agencies, and not-for-profit organizations in the United States take precisely this approach. In doing so, they ignore a solid body of research about how leaders actually develop. This is a curious phenomenon. What is behind it?

The story is complex, but here is a brief, two-part explanation:

1. Training classes and competency instruments are easier to package and sell than strategic conversations about on-the-job learning. This is why the leadership development industry has built itself around training people in competencies—indeed, why it's often called the leadership training industry.

2. The people in organizations who typically see themselves as owning leadership development, HR staff, have limited political and institutional power. If leadership development were built around on-the-job experience, they might have even less because the key decisions (who to hire and what assignments to give them) are owned by line managers, not HR. This is why even the most effective current leadership development offering, action learning (which involves high potential leaders from across an organization making recommendations about real strategic issues) is still typically viewed as a program with some degree of artificiality rather than a genuine on-the-job experience.

HOW ACCOUNTABLE ARE TOP EXECUTIVES FOR DEVELOPING LEADERSHIP?

Many consultants and coaches I know refuse to accept assignments with organizations unless they are working directly with senior executives. If the person calling them the first time works in human resources, they'll take the call, but if the second conversation isn't with a senior executive, my colleagues aren't interested. Although I use a more flexible approach and do my best to bolster the credibility of skilled HR leaders, I understand why my peers take such a strong stance. If you want to get something done in organizations, it's best to start with senior executives not just endorsing it, but owning it. This is as true for developing leadership as it is for creating new products or entering new markets and countries.

A 2005 report by Hewitt Associates supports this point.[7] The researchers compared how twenty top-performing companies treated leadership development with how other companies in the study handled it. They found that senior leaders in the high-performing companies were significantly more likely to be intensively involved with leadership development:

- In 100 percent of the top twenty companies, the CEO was actively involved in developing talent. This was true in only 65 percent of the other companies.

- In 65 percent of the high performing companies, the Board was actively involved in developing talent. This was true in only 31 percent of the remaining companies.

- In 80 percent of the high performing companies, senior leaders were held accountable through performance management for developing their direct reports. This was true in only 35 percent of the other companies.

- The high performing companies tied a significantly higher percentage of senior leaders' annual performance incentive to the objective of developing their direct reports.

What specifically do top leaders in such companies do to own leadership development? According to the Human Resource Institute,[8] they employ the following strategies, and the more time they spend on these strategies, the greater their success:

- Build their direct reports' capabilities—those required for business strategy—mostly through experience
- Participate in talent reviews
- Mentor up-and-coming leaders
- Teach in leadership development programs
- Approve lower level moves (decisions to move more junior managers to new roles)
- Speak publicly about leadership development

What happens when top leaders are less involved? According to Jay Conger and Robert Fulmer of the USC Center for Effective Organizations:

> Without active commitment at the very top—as well as from the executive team—managers will sense that succession management is a tangential activity, and you won't get consistent and coherent commitment. Instead, you may find that division executives hide and hoard their talent by manipulating their assessments.[9]

Hiding and hoarding talent is the reality in most organizations. And understandably so. Your salary, bonus, promotions, social status, and career depend almost entirely on your performance (and political savvy), not your success at developing people. And if the top executives in your company aren't concerned about developing leaders, why would you be?

In contrast, consider what it's like to work in one of the rare organizations that hold executives accountable for developing people. In *The Talent Masters*, Bill Conaty and Ram Charan tell the story of a senior leader within Unilever's Indian subsidiary:

> Unless you knew him by sight, you wouldn't imagine that the dapper businessman sitting next to you at a restaurant in the small south Indian town of Salem is anybody notable. He is listening attentively as a young manager describes recent work. From overheard snatches, you infer that the young manager is brand-new on the job. The conversation is cordial but intense. The senior executive listens closely and often asks pointed questions. Sometimes he seems satisfied with the reply. At other times he offers advice or probes for more information, drilling down with the seasoned familiarity of an old hand at the business. As you finish your dinner and leave, they are still talking earnestly.

Had you recognized the businessman, however, you might wonder what Nitin Paranjpe, the CEO of mighty Hindustan Unilever (HUL), Unilever's $3.5 billion Indian subsidiary and an increasingly important contributor to its global strategy and success, is doing in this out-of-the-way place talking to some kid. But it's the sort of thing Paranjpe does five or six times a month: he visits young sales managers, many of them management trainees who are HUL's up-and-coming future leaders in the field. So do all HUL senior managers, who spend 30 to 40 percent of their time "growing leaders," as they put it, to meet the company's future challenges.[10]

In sharing this example, I don't mean to hold it up as a model of what it means to develop leaders. Many of the important elements are in place—matching top talent to pivotal roles, investing executive time, asking good questions, and listening—but, if we look closer, we may find that others are missing. I set a high bar for greatness, which will become clear as we explore the practices of great leadership in this book. Nevertheless, this example illustrates the unmistakable benefits of senior executives getting personally involved in leadership development. Although it guarantees neither great leadership development nor great leadership, it provides an important foundation for both.

WHAT ROLES DO MANAGERS PLAY IN DEVELOPING MANAGERS WHO REPORT TO THEM?

The story of Hindustan Unilever illustrates how ownership of leadership development by senior executives can cascade down an organization. The company's CEO is not the only one who spends 30 to 40 percent of his time developing leaders. So, too, do all senior managers in the company. As a result, managers at every level get challenged and supported by their own bosses to maximize what they learn from their experiences.

This matches another important research finding: in organizations that do the best job cultivating leadership, managers take personal responsibility for developing their direct reports, and this happens on the job. What specific actions do they take to develop their direct reports? An illuminating new study by Jeannie Coyle and Wendy Axelrod provides an answer. Coyle and Axelrod searched well-known companies for exceptional development managers, people who "truly develop the capacity of their employees beyond day-to-day performance needs."[11] After interviewing these managers and employees who reported to them, they discovered five common practices of exceptional development managers. As summarized in *Make Talent Your Business*, these practices are to:

1. Make every day a development day by creating stretches for employees, tucking development into everyday work, providing effective feedback, and turning mistakes into learning opportunities.

2. Tap the psychological side of development by building their own self-awareness, cultivating relationships built on trust, and helping employees "see" themselves during key interactions.

3. Connect people with development partners. First, identify *what* employees need to learn, then identify *who* can help them learn these things, and finally contract for *how* the learning will occur.

4. Teach skills to navigate organizational politics by adjusting assumptions about politics, mapping the bumpy political terrain, coaching employees to build a portfolio of savvy approaches, and helping them prepare for complex situations.

5. Shape their environment to drive development by cycling great learning experiences between employees, rewarding development, and creating political cover for hiring employees based not only

on who has the best experience, but also on who can learn the most from the job.[12]

This is an extraordinary set of practices. Have you ever had a manager who used some of them in managing you? What was that like? I imagine that your experience reporting to this person was both challenging and highly engaging. And I bet you learned a ton.

Now, contrast this experience with jobs you've had reporting to managers who did not actively support your development. What was it like to work for someone who didn't pay attention to what you were learning? How much did you grow? How much better did you get at managing or leading?

Finally, I invite you to turn the mirror on yourself. How much attention have you placed on developing the people who report to you? How has this affected the ability of your employees to grow through their on-the-job experiences?

As we explore these tough questions, I hope that one thing becomes clear: there is a large gap between what exceptional development managers do to develop their direct reports and what most managers do. When these direct reports are themselves managers, the impact on leadership development is even more substantial.

In summary, if we want to develop great leadership, we can start by mimicking or at least learning from the best leadership development approaches. We can:

1. Develop leadership through on-the-job experience by matching talented managers who can learn with challenging experiences that teach pivotal lessons.

2. Ensure that top executives take personal ownership of developing leadership.

3. Challenge and support managers at every level to get actively involved in developing their direct reports.

If we do these three things, the quality of leadership will rise more than most of us can imagine. Employees will be more engaged. Work will be more focused and relevant. Customers and clients will receive more value. And the pipeline of leaders that carries tomorrow's executives will be more robust.

All of this can happen not by doing what's popular, but by doing what works. American pragmatism at its best.

Yet, even this is not the whole story.

The field of leadership development is a wonderful source of guidance about developing great leadership, but it is not the only one. We can also look *outside* this field for clues. When I did this myself, I discovered the best practical wisdom in a most unusual place: the hotbeds of high performance in sports, music, and the performing arts. The people who work in these hotbeds don't identify primarily as leaders, but what they do to succeed offers important insights for leaders. The people who study these hotbeds don't talk a lot about business or organization, but the secrets that they've uncovered are highly relevant to organizational success.

What specific approaches do these talent hotbeds use to grow world-class performers? Why don't we hear a lot about these approaches in books and classes about leadership? If your organization decided to adapt these approaches to its own efforts to develop leadership, what might this look like—and what positive results might ensue? These questions are the focus of the next chapter.

CHAPTER 3
LESSONS FROM TALENT HOTBEDS

"MANY OF US view practice as necessary drudgery, the equivalent of being forced to eat your vegetables, far less important or interesting than the big game or the big performance. But in the talent hotbeds I visited, practice *was* the big game, the center of their world, the main focus of their daily lives. This approach succeeds because over time, practice is transformative, if it's the right kind of practice. Deep practice."

—Daniel Coyle, *The Little Book of Talent*

In competitive sports, music, and the theatrical arts, people spend far more time preparing for performances than they do performing. They call this practice, and they do it for a simple reason: to get better. In many sports, athletes and their coaches devote large chunks of time to reviewing video footage of their performances. In football, some say that watching game film is half of coaching.[13]

Might there be a lesson in this for organizations investing in leadership development? I suspect there is. But, first, let's consider a question that rarely gets asked: Why *do* athletes, musicians, and theatrical artists practice? Why don't they rely solely on performance to get better? Wouldn't this save a lot of time?

Here are two major reasons:

1. *A strict focus on performance limits learning—and vice versa.* The goal of performance is to be your best or to win. The goal of practice is to learn and improve. You can and will learn while performing, but if learning is your emphasis, your performance may plummet. Do you practice your layup when your team is down by three points with two seconds to play? Ever seen a PGA golfer take a mulligan in the middle of a round to practice his golf swing? Better yet, ever seen a ballet dancer stop mid-performance to repeat a move? These things generally don't happen during performances. They happen during practice.

2. *There are logistical hurdles to learning while performing.* Many forms of practice cannot happen within a performance because they don't fit logistically. Consider one way that musicians practice. You break the skill (composition) into its parts, practice each part with intent, and get feedback from a teacher. A cellist who did this while performing would quickly lose her audience. Or consider the chess model of practice. You study situations faced by masters of the skill, decide which moves you would make, and compare your moves to theirs. In an actual game of chess, there isn't time for this. Finally, consider the sports conditioning model of practice. You lift weights, run track intervals, and ride the stationary bike to build the underlying muscles and stamina needed to perform at a high level. Carrying a dumbbell onto a soccer field during a game would be awkward and dangerous. That's why we have weight rooms.

Given how much time competitive athletes, musicians, and theatrical artists spend practicing, you would expect people in organizations to schedule time for practice, too. In fact, you would assume that the highest performing people in the roles with the greatest influence on an organization's success would be practicing the most. Their bosses (or Board) would demand it, and their compensation would depend upon it. Surely this is how things work, right?

Not at all. People in twenty-first century organizations don't practice. They just perform. Working for nine hours means performing for nine hours. Practice is not included. Even the very activities that are supposed to produce learning—training—often contain very little actual hands-on practice. As a result, it is not uncommon to find people who are devoted to practice outside of work but wouldn't think of practicing while at work. Consider, for example, the VP of Marketing who excels at golf. For every round of golf she plays, she makes several visits to the driving range and putting green to practice her strokes. Yet if you ask her which pivotal meetings she rehearses for in advance, her answer is a blank wordless stare. *Practice for a meeting. What, are you kidding?*

Isn't it curious that we wouldn't dare play competitive sports without practicing yet we also wouldn't even consider practicing in the workplace?

Actually, it's quite normal, and that's the point.

First, the bad news. It's highly likely that:

- You've received little support or direction in your career about practicing leadership.

- Your manager neither expects you to practice nor is supportive of it.

- Your organization isn't going to reward you for it—at least not directly.

- You don't have the foggiest idea of what practicing leadership would look like.

Now, the good news:

- Since nobody else is practicing leadership, you don't have to catch up. In fact, you can get ahead. Perform better by practicing more.

- There is a specific set of practices that are designed to raise your game. They are practical, actionable, and targeted at evoking greatness. This book describes fifteen such practices.

- Most forms of practice don't require extra time. You can do them during your regular work experience and by cutting out time-wasting activities.

- In this book, I give you very specific tips about how to practice. You can start using them today.

WHAT IS DELIBERATE PRACTICE?

Let's begin by defining what we mean by deliberate (as opposed to accidental or unfocused) practice. In *Talent is Overrated*, Fortune magazine senior editor Geoff Colvin describes the ingredients of deliberate practice:

- It is designed specifically to improve performance.
- It can be repeated at high volume.
- The person receives continuous feedback from a teacher or coach.
- It requires intense focus and concentration.
- It may not always be fun.[14]

In *The Talent Code*, Daniel Coyle writes that high performers often break skills into chunks, practice the chunks slowly, and correct mistakes along the way.[15]

As you consider these descriptions, what experiences from your own life come to mind? Perhaps music lessons or sports practice as a kid. You called it *practice* to distinguish it from a game or live performance. Or how about the way you learned technical skills in your formal education and early career? These activities likely included many, if not all, of the elements of deliberate practice.

Now, consider how you practice your work today. Whether you are officially a manager or you practice leadership in a non-managerial capacity, how have you improved at what you do? Can you recall any times that you've deliberately practiced management or leadership? Any opportunities to repeatedly practice a leadership skill in order to improve performance? Any on-the-job experiences or classes in which you received live feedback about your leadership from a manager or coach?

The answer to these questions for most of us is no. We haven't deliberately practiced leadership—or even been invited to do so. In fact, the very idea of deliberately practicing leadership seems unfamiliar, even bizarre. The reason for this isn't that we haven't wanted to improve. We have! Unfortunately, the field of leadership development—and all of the companies within it that sell and use services—hasn't done a good job of supporting this intention. The best methods for fostering high performance in leadership have not been available. Bosses have not modeled deliberate practice, and organizations have neither encouraged nor created space for it.

Deliberate practice is the most effective method of evoking high performance yet it is almost completely absent from the field of leadership development.

WHY IS DELIBERATE PRACTICE A FOREIGN CONCEPT INSIDE OF ORGANIZATIONS?

What's going on here? Why do organizations that invest millions of dollars in developing leadership pay so little attention to the research on high performance in sports, music, and the theatrical arts? And why does that VP of Marketing who diligently practices golf look puzzled when asked to describe the last time she rehearsed for a pivotal executive meeting?

One explanation is inertia. Organizations have never encouraged deliberate practice. However, organizations are continually trying out new ways of developing leaders—often to a fault. The phrase "flavor-of-the-month" refers to the phenomenon of an executive or HR leader going to a seminar, getting excited about a new model for organizational change or leadership development, and then asking everyone in the organization to learn it. This happens all the time. Why isn't deliberate practice, at the very minimum, one of these flavors-of-the-month?

It's a case of siloing. The people writing books and leading seminars about leadership development aren't talking about deliberate practice or tapping the research on high performance. And the people writing books and leading seminars about high performance through deliberate practice aren't exploring the applications to leadership. For example, Malcolm Gladwell's *Outliers* talks at length about Bill Gates' use of practice, but as a programmer who practiced coding, not an entrepreneur who practiced leading.[16] Similarly, *The Talent Code* contains only two pages on business, and it's in the epilogue. Why is there this big gap between the research on high performance outside the field of management and the best expertise within the field of management?

I see five explanations:

1. *Talent researchers aren't interested in management.* Most psychologists, neuroscientists, and journalists (even those writing about business) don't have managerial experience, nor have they spent

much time in their careers watching managers in action. In contrast, all have been through school and most have played sports or a musical instrument. They study what they know.

2. *Management researchers generally don't focus on individual practices.* There are thousands of books written about the attributes of great leaders. However, few focus in an actionable way on deliberate managerial practices.

3. *Deliberate managerial practices are difficult to study.* If you want to learn how people get good at soccer or the violin, you can go to the talent hotbeds for these disciplines and watch what happens. The teachers and heads of schools are often willing to let you watch, particularly if you're going to write a best-selling book. And sometimes you don't even need their permission. For example, you can learn how Brazilian kids get great at soccer by watching them play Futsall, a mini-version of soccer that involves a small heavy ball, a tiny field, and non-stop action. But management is very different. It happens inside of organizations: in one-on-one meetings between managers and their direct reports, in team discussions, in Board rooms, on construction sites, in wet labs, and on factory floors. The people working in these places are neither accustomed to having outsiders watch them, nor comfortable with being studied.

4. *Management researchers may not know what to observe.* Managers live in the world of language—speaking, listening, and facial and body expressions. If you want to understand what they are practicing, you have to understand the distinctions—the vocabularies— within each of these domains and have the observational skills to know what you are seeing. For example, if you're watching a sales team discuss how to talk with their biggest customer about a delivery delay, what do you look for? What is the equivalent in a team conversation of the various dribbling moves of a soccer

player or the pattern-recognition of a chess master? If you were videotaping the scene, what would you capture on film that could tell you whether the team was having this conversation at a mediocre, good, or great level? If you cannot answer this question, it's hard to tell a story about what excellence looks like, much less propose ways to get there. Fortunately, there is a robust and detailed grammar of how we bring about action through language. It's the terrain of speech acts or promise-based management. On a micro-level, you can look at the power of declarations made in the meeting, the ability of the team to ground their assessments, the reliability of promises, and the clarity of requests. These are all highly specific and highly actionable. Unfortunately, this grammar remains relatively unknown in the world of management writing outside of the students of Fernando Flores, who first introduced these concepts into organizational settings. Similarly, if you want to describe how the physical presence and body language of the team contributed to or detracted from their success, you can tap into the grammar of somatic intelligence, as described by Richard Strozzi-Heckler, Wendy Palmer and Janet Crawford, and Barbara and Alan Pease, or the anatomy of microscopic facial expressions, as detailed by Paul Ekman. However, these distinctions, too, remain mostly outside of mainstream management writing, which generally treat managers as disembodied creatures (i.e. brains with laptops and smart phones).

5. *Few organizations offer deliberate management practices.* Ultimately, it's difficult to study something that isn't happening. Most organizations don't consciously challenge managers to practice managing either on the job or in formal training. The closest they come to this is selecting on-the-job experiences that are likely to teach managers what they need to learn, but this occurs only within a few select talent machines. Even these organizations rarely show managers how to break down the skills that these

experiences can teach into their component parts or replicate any of the other techniques found on Brazilian soccer fields and in elite music camps.

BUILDING LEADERSHIP DEVELOPMENT AROUND DELIBERATE PRACTICE AND ON-THE-JOB EXPERIENCE

There is an extraordinary business opportunity for organizations that takes these points seriously and decide to embed the rules of deliberate practice into their leadership development. The opportunity is this: your organization will develop managers faster and better than anyone else. Accomplishing this will require thinking in radically new ways about leadership development. Many organizations won't be up for this challenge because it seems risky or threatens existing power structures and cultural assumptions. But those organizations that take deliberate practice seriously will yield enormous benefits in the form of vastly higher quality leadership. And they'll realize that the risks of modeling leadership development after the development of talent in other fields are far less than the risks of continuing the ineffective approaches they use today.

What might this look like? Organizations building leadership development around deliberate practice, while also capturing the value of on-the-job learning, will:

1. Encourage leaders to focus on a small set of leadership skills that are actionable and practicable. Actionable means that they're described specifically enough that they can be performed. Practicable means that they are something you can deliberately practice. In this book, I refer to these skills as the practices of great leadership.

2. Support leaders in identifying a small number of practices that will make the biggest difference in improving their leadership.

3. Make sure that at least one of these practices is *outer* (related to external behaviors like speaking, listening, and having conversations) and one is *inner* (focused on what makes the leader tick and other patterns of thinking and feeling that lay beneath their behaviors).

4. Create a specific method of practicing these on the job so that leaders can get the most value from on-the-job experience.

5. Select on-the-job experiences that teach leaders the specific lessons they need to learn to succeed in bigger roles in the future.

6. Give managers incentives and support for developing the managers who report to them.

7. Have senior executives take personal responsibility for owning and modeling leadership development.

This strategy of combining deliberate practice with on-the-job learning in order to cultivate great leadership has the potential to radically shift how organizations develop their people. The promise is development of better leaders faster and creation of organizational cultures that sustain such development in the future. The reason this strategy *can* work is that it is based on approaches that *do* work. Indeed, like much innovation, it taps the best research from within its own field and also incorporates ideas from other fields.

Now that we've explored *how* to develop great leadership, you may be wondering *what* specific practices constitute great leadership. If you are ready to raise your game, have a manager who is invested in your development, and have a CEO who personally owns leadership development in the organization, what specifically can you practice to improve your leadership? Most of the remainder of the book is devoted to answering this question.

But, first, we will address another issue: what can get in the way of using practice to develop great leadership in your organization. I could save this issue for the end of the book in order to postpone the unpleasantries. However, most of this mud and muck is already familiar to you. If we address it head on at the outset, you'll know that I know *how things really are.* Once we agree that life inside your organization isn't all puppy dogs and ice cream, we can turn our attention to how we can make it better.

CHAPTER 4
OBSTACLES TO PRACTICING GREATNESS

"AT THE TIME this nation was formed, our population stood at around 3 million. And we produced out of that 3 million people perhaps six leaders of world class: Washington, Adams, Jefferson, Franklin, Madison, and Hamilton. Today, our population stands at 245 million, so we might expect at least 80 times as many world-class leaders: 480 Jeffersons, Madisons, Adamses, Washingtons, Hamiltons, and Franklins. Where are they?"

—John W. Gardner, *On Leadership*

In an ideal world, all of the conditions that support great leadership would be in place. Your boss would encourage your growth and spend time each week reviewing what you learned. The top executives in your organization would model great leadership and foster it in others. Your colleagues would be as committed to elevating their game as you are.

And your compensation would depend not only on how you perform, but also on how much you learn and how much you help others develop.

That's the ideal world.

In *our* world, you can count yourself as fortunate if even one of these conditions is in place. This is because our world is inhabited largely by fear-based organizations. A fear-based organization is one in which people spend a disproportionate amount of time feeling anxious about their jobs, their careers, their friendships, and their overall security, and don't feel safe talking about these anxieties. As a result, these fears get lodged in their bodies and show up every day as unskillful behaviors, unhealthy cultures, and distrustful systems and structures. In these organizations, criticism trumps appreciation and control systems waste time and drain human energy.

Nearly everyone I know has at some point worked in a fear-based organization. Some enter hoping to have a positive experience, then discover that things are "really screwed up" and get out as fast as they can. Others who experience a similar hope/disappointment cycle nonetheless stick it out for months, years, or even decades. Still others sign on with a sober awareness of what's coming because the pay and benefits are good, the company is an industry leader, the geographical location works, or a close friend works there.

Regardless of the situation, it's quite challenging to practice greatness in such organizations. The reason, as Peter Drucker taught us, is that culture eats strategy for breakfast. In fear-based cultures, it's not just hard to enact bold new organizational strategies, it's also difficult to employ personal strategies to become the best version of yourself. The entire system—from written policies and incentives to unwritten codes of behavior—gets in the way. This is one reason that my colleagues in the leadership development field have a saying: never send a changed person back to an unchanged organization. It is also a reason why, if you want to practice greatness yet happen to work in a fear-based culture, it's important to take a sober look at that culture. What obstacles to practicing leadership tend to come with the territory in a fear-based organization? Identifying these obstacles is important even if you lack the power to remove or change them. By being aware of what gets in the way of leading with your best, you can adjust what and how you practice to produce more learning with less anguish. Or, in some cases, you may find that the obstacles are so substantial that it's time to leave the organization or at least switch to another part of it.

What, then, are the obstacles to practicing greatness in a fear-based organization? In my experience coaching and developing leaders, I've seen three obstacles show up with great regularity:

1. Managing through fear

2. Managing performance through forced ranking

3. Overscheduling

Interestingly, even in organizations that I would not strictly label as fear-based, people complain about these same three things. And these things get in the way of initiating and sustaining deliberate leadership practices. That's why I think of them as quasi-universal obstacles to practicing great leadership. As I describe them in more detail, you may find yourself nodding with recognition.

MANAGING THROUGH FEAR

As a management approach, trying to accomplish things by evoking fear yields poor results. Research on employee engagement shows that:

*   There is a strong correlation between employee engagement and productivity, customer engagement, quality, retention, safety, and profit. Studies by Gallup involving millions of employees around the world make this connection crystal clear.[17]

- Employees become dramatically less engaged when their bodies experience the threat ("fight, flight, or freeze") response. In the words of consultant David Rock, who uses brain research to rethink management practices, "because the [threat] response uses up oxygen and glucose from the blood, they are diverted from other parts of the brain, including the working memory function, which processes new information and ideas. This impairs analytic thinking, creative insight, and problem solving."[18]

- Triggering another person's threat response is not hard to do. All it takes is managing in a way that keeps employees from experiencing five social qualities: status, certainty, autonomy, relatedness, and fairness. Rock calls these the SCARF qualities. An employee whose status has been challenged or autonomy stripped away reacts the same way physiologically as if someone were pointing a gun at them. People who use fear to manage therefore have to try really hard to *not* trigger others' threat responses.

If your boss manages through fear—and it never ceases to amaze me how many senior executives at top companies do—you will use a lot of energy avoiding your boss and trying to placate him. You likely will also take fewer personal risks, focus more on performance than learning (even though the former requires the latter), hide mistakes rather than using them to improve, and push away the very feedback that could help you improve. And here's the ultimate irony: even if you don't believe in managing through fear, you may find yourself mimicking your boss because that's what he and the organization reward.

All of these things that a fear-based boss brings into your life have a consequence. They substantially increase the odds that you will forget your own greatness. The idea that you could develop to your full potential, much less harness this for a greater good, becomes an elusive if not laughable proposition. As a result, you are unlikely to identify the skills you need to develop to be a better leader and are even less likely to deliberately practice these skills.

Unless, that is, you see these circumstances with a clear mind and an open heart and dedicate yourself to a path of growth regardless of who or what gets in your way.

MANAGING PERFORMANCE VIA FORCED RANKING

Even if you don't work for someone who leads through fear, you may encounter other dimensions of a fear-based culture. One of the more pernicious of these is employee performance management, particularly the type that ranks people, including managers, against each other. GE has used such a system for years and done quite well as a company. However, it's not clear whether their success is because or in spite of forced ranking. If you work at GE, your manager places you in one of three categories: high performer (the top 20%), middle performer (the middle 70%), or low performer (the bottom 10%). If you're a low performer, you get removed or improved. Sounds like meritocracy at its best, right? Not really. As USC management professor, John Boudreau, points out:

> Is removing or improving the bottom 10 percent valuable in all cases? Certainly in some situations even the bottom 10 percent are doing an adequate job and are doing better than those who could be hired or promoted. By definition, continually removing or improving the bottom 10 percent will make the bottom 10 percent more similar to the middle 70 percent and thus make removing the bottom 10 percent less effective in improving workforce quality.[19]

What about companies that rank employees but don't automatically remove people? A clue may come from Microsoft. After years of extraordinary success, the company stumbled during the decade after the year 2000. A cover story in the August 2012 issue of *Vanity Fair* explores why. The author, Kurt Eichenwald, reveals a startling discovery:

> Every current and former Microsoft employee I interviewed—*every one*—cited stack ranking as the most destructive process inside of Microsoft...

> "The behavior this engenders, people do everything they can to stay out of the bottom bucket," one Microsoft engineer said. "People responsible for features will openly sabotage other people's efforts. One of the most valuable things I learned was to give the appearance of being courteous while withholding just enough information from colleagues to ensure they didn't get ahead of me on the rankings."

> Worse, because the reviews came every six months, employees and their supervisors—who were also ranked—focused on their short-term performance, rather than on longer efforts to innovate.

> "The six-month reviews forced a lot of bad decision-making," one software designer said. "People planned their days and their years around the review, rather than around products. You really had to focus on the six-month performance, rather than on doing what was right for the company."[20]

The article emphasizes the impact of ranking systems on performance and does so for good reason. Like many artifacts of a fear-based culture, ranking systems waste extraordinary amounts of time. As a manager you spend time proposing rank orders and debating them with others. You spend time worrying about how you're going to explain to a perfectly competent employee that they are below average. You spend time meeting with employees. And you spend more time in subsequent weeks and months dealing with the emotional fallout. As an employee being ranked, the time sink is the effort it takes to position yourself with your boss, your boss's boss, and your boss's boss's peers so that you can look good in what is largely a political game. Even if you enjoy this game, it has a cost: the time you spend on performance reviews is time you are not spending on activities that add real value to the organization, not to mention those that grow your skills.[21]

Thus, ranking systems don't just interfere with performance. They also get in the way of learning.

In companies that employ such a system—and I've worked with several—people spend performance review month in a mood of resignation. They go to all the same meetings and have all the same conversations, but with a bit less energy and a lot less enthusiasm. It's not that they cannot tolerate the system or don't know how to navigate through it. Instead, it's that they despise and resent it even while believing there is nothing they can do about it.

People who are bummed out and feel resigned about the future are unlikely to have the energy to invest in developing themselves or others. This is why, when I'm working in such an organization, I attempt to bring this issue to the forefront first:

Senior leader: Amiel, as you know, we are trying to make a major strategic change over the next three years, and we'd love your help thinking about how to develop our leaders for this. What can we do that's truly impactful?

Me: I'd enjoy having that conversation. But first there is something I'm curious about. You want to develop leaders who can collaborate on teams and across divisional lines, but your ranking system forces them to compete with each other—plus it sucks up a lot of time. Have you considered taking a look at that system and, say, getting rid of it?

Senior leader: Well, now that you mention it, we are experimenting with de-emphasizing rankings.

Me: Really, what do you mean?

Senior leader: One of our smaller departments is trying this out for a year and if it goes well, we'll try it elsewhere.

Me: What's the timeframe on that?

Senior leader: Not sure, but I'd guess over the next three or four years.

Me [thinking but not saying]: Gee, love the general direction, but if boldness and speed are the company's mantras, what don't you toss the whole thing out soon—say, next Monday?

So far, nobody has terminated my contract for talking like this. On the other hand, I haven't seen much movement to dismantle the performance ranking system.[22] That's unfortunate, because when it's gone, a great deal of energy is unleashed for practicing greatness.

OVERSCHEDULING

The days of back-to-back meetings have ended. Managers now live in an era of back-to-back-to-back-to-back meetings—and that's on a light day! If you had to custom design a schedule that would shrink people's moods and suck out their energy, you couldn't design one better than the back-to-back-to-back-to-back. In fact, research shows that high performers in every field do exactly the opposite. They go through a perform-renew-perform-renew cycle that gives them a break every 90 minutes.[23] But this does not occur in most organizations, and certainly not in fear-based cultures.

Now, you might think that all these meetings are a good idea. Rather than sitting at their desks, managers are out talking with employees and each other. They're getting things done together, rather than alone. Isn't that what collaboration is all about?

I once asked this to an executive I was coaching. His response: "Hell no!"

Managers waste enormous amounts of time in meetings. You know this. You've complained about it. Everyone you know has complained about it. I want to convince you that it doesn't have to be that way—and, as I'll discuss in the chapter "Managing Commitments," that there are practical steps you can take to free yourself from meeting-overload.

But first, I'd like to describe the managerial habits that cause overscheduling:

- *Scheduling meetings that don't have to happen.* This includes everything from work groups and task forces that lack a clear purpose to standing meetings that have lost their rationale for being.

- *Scheduling meetings for more time than you need.* Parkinson's Law says that "work expands so as to fill the time available for its completion." The longer you schedule a meeting, the more time you'll spend in that meeting.

- *Wasting time in the meetings you do attend.* Have you ever calculated the percentage of meeting time that adds value (productive conversations about important topics) versus the percentage that is wasteful (unfocused conversations, tangential topics, and unnecessary conflict)? Waste consumes a big piece of the pie.

- *Assuming you need to be at every meeting.* "If I don't go, I may miss something important." Or so you think. Have you ever actually calculated the cost of missing something? Simply multiply the cost of the missed experience by the probability of that experience occurring in your absence. Now compare that to the opportunity cost of *not* accomplishing something else instead of attending that meeting. Which cost is larger?

- *Being physically present—and absent in every other way.* Because you are afraid of missing something, you go to a meeting. But because you really don't need to be there and have other things to do, you work on your laptop most of the time. You might even send an email to the person sitting next to you in the meeting working on her laptop. If all goes well, she'll whisper back to you, "Thanks for the email. You saved my butt on that one."

- *Assuming other managers need to be at meetings you have called.* There is great value in ensuring that conversations reflect a wide range of perspectives. Excluding people for the sake of excluding them is a lousy practice. That's not what we're talking about here. My point is that you may be inviting more people to meetings than are needed, either to add value or to ensure a feeling of inclusion. Said differently, when other managers attend your meetings when their time would produce greater value elsewhere, you own part of the responsibility for their wasted time.

Overscheduling has several negative impacts on leaders. First, it makes them tired. As mentioned above, non-stop performing reduces performance because the body needs opportunities throughout the day to renew. Second, it reduces the amount of time that leaders have to manage their other commitments. This includes both the commitments they have to themselves (as captured in action lists, project folders, and so on) and the promises they have made to others. As a result, how do leaders use the spare moments they have at lunchtime, at the end of the day, or (as so often happens) at night or on the weekend? Simply trying to catch up. After all, they reason, time is scarce, and every free moment needs to be spent fulfilling basic obligations.

It's hard to argue with this logic. Devoting your limited time to meeting current commitments makes a lot of sense. It's what responsible people do. However, there is a cost. When you spend one hundred percent of your day performing—and none of it deliberately practicing new skills—it's very difficult to become a better leader. As we will see later in the book, on-the-job practice requires, among other things, preparation (for conversations, meetings, projects, and reviews) and reflection (on what went well, what you could do better, and what new possibilities you see). Both preparation and reflection take time—far less than you might think, but still some—so cutting them out means substantially lowering the odds of realizing your greatness.

This is why I like to stick my head in my clients' calendars from time to time. Naturally, we do it together, but it doesn't happen unless I request it. That's why I say I "stick my head" in their calendars. It is an unusual act. Other than my clients and their executive assistants, nobody looks closely at these leaders' calendars. This is strange, because their calendars provide a powerful window into where they are placing—and not placing—their attention.

When we look at calendars, here are some of the questions we ask:

- Which meetings did you call? What purposes do they serve? Is there another way to accomplish these purposes? If not, what topics could be taken out of these meetings or done more quickly? What happens during them that you would call waste? What if you were to shorten the meetings, postpone them, or hold them less often? What if you were to make a deal with participants: if you give me one hundred percent of your attention (no electronic devices), then I'll reduce the meeting time in half?

- Which meetings are on your calendar but you don't know why they are? Is it possible that you were invited accidentally, as a courtesy, or to avoid offending you or your boss? What's the next action you can take to answer these questions?

- Which meetings might provide good developmental opportunities to your staff? Is it really essential that you show up or could you delegate leading these meetings to them?

These questions invite people to make individual changes in how they manage their calendars. However, they don't address the issues from a system-wide perspective. Even if you do everything you can to use your meeting time wisely, a great deal of your calendar may still be outside your sphere of influence. This is an organizational issue that calls for an organizational response. For this reason, the challenge of back-to-back-to-back-to-back meetings belongs on the radar of senior executives and their HR partners—not just when talking about management development or organizational health, but also when discussing how to achieve the organization's most vital strategic priorities.

A CREATIVE RESPONSE TO OBSTACLES

In this chapter, we've walked together through the mud and muck of fear-based organizations. The situation isn't pretty, but it's ours. We can choose whether to ignore it, resent it, or design creative responses to it.

I vote for the creative path. It's the only option that increases our freedom and power while also keeping us connected to the actual world that we inhabit.

For some people, a creative response to these expressions of fear-based cultures will include actively trying to change them. For example, you may dedicate yourself to wielding greater influence in who becomes a manager, so that people who rule by fear are less likely to get hired. (Hint: start with managers of managers, because they decide which individual contributors enter the managerial ranks.) Or you can position yourself to have a say in how—or whether—your organization conducts performance reviews. Or maybe you'll use your leverage to radically shift how scheduling happens, if not in the entire organization then at least within your division or team. We need more leaders who are willing to use their political capital to make significant changes like these. The risks are high, but so are the rewards.

For others, creatively responding to a fear-based culture will mean bringing greater care and savvy to selecting what to practice and how to practice it. The idea is to devote your energy and attention in such a way that you can become better at what you do no matter what gets in your way. You have a fear-driven boss? Not fun, but also no reason to despair. You can actually use this hardship as a learning opportunity. You can practice *turning toward* your boss and *listening like a master* for her concerns (two of the practices I'll introduce) even when she's in a foul mood. You're stuck in a forced ranking performance system? Bummer, but you can view it as an invitation to *tell powerful stories, make peace with your enemies,* or *hold conversations for possibility* (three other practices that I'll introduce). Your organization's policies make it difficult to unclutter your calendar? You can interpret this as a reason to get better at *keeping commitments to yourself* (so you can make good use of the free time you do have) or *increasing your physical energy* (so your body and mind can stay fresh even amidst a packed schedule).

What's at stake here is nothing less than your ability to grow to your full potential. Rather than being mastered by your context, you take the initiative to master your context. By doing this, you create the conditions for your own greatness to arise. This is why it pays to understand the difference between on-the-job learning and formal training. Why it makes sense to adapt the best lessons from talent hotbeds outside of leadership to your own life. And, why it is important to develop skillful responses to the forces of a fear-based culture.

This brings us to the topic of the next chapter: introducing the practices of great leadership. It's one thing to be serious about raising your game and quite another to have a clear vision of the practices required to do so. As we've seen, great leadership means realizing your full potential for the sake of a purpose larger than yourself. What specifically does this mean for you? What leadership practices will provide the greatest leverage toward realizing your potential?

CHAPTER 5

15 PRACTICES OF GREAT LEADERSHIP

"WE ARE WHAT we repeatedly do. Excellence, then, is not an act, but a habit."

—Aristotle

The research on leadership development and high performance provides us with sound guidance. If you want to foster great leadership, match capable people who possess high learning agility with on-the-job experiences that teach pivotal lessons—and engage them in long-term deliberate practice, like they do in talent hotbeds. If you want to do this really well, integrate what people learn on the job with the skills they deliberately practice. And ensure that their boss and the top executives in the organization model and encourage such development.

So far, so good. But something is missing.

In fact, two things are missing. Here is what the research on leadership development and high performance does not tell us:

1. What are the specific actionable skills that, when practiced both directly and on the job, are most likely to help leaders realize their full potential for the sake of a larger purpose? In short, what are the practices of great leadership?

2. How can individual leaders (and the managers and coaches who support them) select the one or two practices that will have the largest impact on their leadership? What is their greatest source of leverage?

There is a reason why research has not addressed these questions: the subjects of such research don't exist or are too few in number to study! Do you know any organizations consciously and strategically applying the elements of deliberate practice to the task of developing leadership? I don't. Maybe they're all around us but just really quiet about it.

I'm not alone in this assessment. Consider what famed leadership author Jim Collins says about Level 5 leaders, those capable of guiding organizations from good to great. It turns out that such leaders have an unusual blend of ambition for their organizations and deep personal humility. But how does Collins suggest a person actually develop such capabilities? Here's what he says:

> For your own development, I would love to be able to give you a list of steps for becoming Level 5, but we have no solid research data that would support a credible list. Our research exposed Level 5 as a key component inside the black box of what it takes to shift a company from good to great. Yet inside that black box is yet another black box—namely, the inner development of a person to Level 5. We could speculate on what might be inside that inner black box, but it would mostly be just that—speculation.[24]

Fortunately, the lack of solid data isn't the end of the story—not ours, at least. Jim Collins is a (wonderful) researcher. Through the eyes of research, proposing a list of steps for great leadership would be speculation. But I am not a researcher nor, in all likelihood, are you. We are players on the field. Different rules apply.

For us, there is another name for creating a list of practices that is not grounded in solid research data: *invention.*

We are inventing a new way of developing leadership.

That's why if you ask me where these practices of great leadership came from, I'll tell you that I invented them—not the practices themselves, but their placement in this book. They did not come from a research study. They emerged from two decades of experience as a consultant and coach combined with conversations with insightful colleagues and a lot of self-study. These are the data sets from which the list of great leadership practices arises. As it turns out, when leaders deliberately take on these practices, they become more self-aware, more powerful, more emotionally intelligent, more politically astute, and more influential in their organizations. In my experience, these practices help leaders realize their full potential.

Now, there is an irony worth mentioning. Even though my method of selecting practices is not grounded in research, nearly all of the individual practices themselves are. For example, the practice of improving relationships by *turning toward* others is based on substantial research by John Gottman and his colleagues at the University of Washington. Likewise, the notion of emergent organizational strategies, a core part of *seeing patterns*, comes from longitudinal studies of successful companies by Henry Mintzberg, the "Peter Drucker of Canada." Finally, the ideas that I share for *increasing physical energy* are based on scientific studies in a wide range of disciplines.

So, to be precise, this book is less an act of invention than an act of *integration.* It integrates ideas and practices from inside and outside the field of leadership development. The principle is simple: look for what works.

Or, to put it differently: Take the best, and jettison the rest.

The best practices for developing leaders fall into two categories:

1. External behaviors that others can see.

2. The internal thoughts, feelings, intentions, and assumptions that often underlie these behaviors and are in turn reinforced by them.

Practices of Great Leadership = External Practices + Internal Practices

Our exploration of practices begins the way most of my coaching engagements begin: with the external practices. What people do and how they do it—these are the places my clients place the bulk of their attention. Behaviors are visible, tangible, and sometimes measurable. We are comfortable talking about them. Or at least more comfortable than we are discussing the inner realm of feelings, intentions, and assumptions. This is true even though some of our largest epiphanies in life, the insights that prompt big behavioral changes, involve what's inside of us. For this reason, although we will devote substantial attention to inner practices, we will start by exploring the *outer* practices of great leadership:

- Hold *conversations for possibility* where what if trumps what could go wrong.

- Build trust in moment-to-moment interactions by *turning toward* other people rather than away from or against them.

- Channel negative energy into positive energy by *flipping complaints into commitments*.

- Evoke possibility amidst disagreement by *arguing better* and *making peace with enemies*.

- Help people see themselves as protagonists in a positive future by *telling powerful stories*.

- Develop the single competence that underlies all of the others—*listening like a master*.

- Generate better stuff to listen to by *asking great questions*.

These outer practices hold great potential for helping you grow as a leader and as a person. There is a lot to learn about them, and you could spend a lifetime learning these things. However, I think you'll find it easier to get traction as you take on any given outer practice, when you simultaneously take on at least one *inner practice* of great leadership. These inner practices complement the outer practices in the way that exercise complements nutrition in losing weight. So I encourage you to consider these inner practices:

- *Visualize* a future you desire.

- Discover organizational strategies and discern human strengths by *seeing patterns*.

- Focus like a laser beam on your greatest weakness by *healing your Achilles' heel*.

- Catch yourself in delusions of grandeur by *calling B.S. on yourself*.

- Get all of this done without adding to your stress by *managing commitments*.

- Become more resilient to life's stresses and challenges by *managing your physical energy*.

- Ensure that you are well positioned for great leadership by *posturing* (which is more physical and less political than it sounds).

CHAPTER 6
IGNITE WITH PURPOSE

"IT'S NOT ENOUGH to have lived. We should be determined to live for something."
—Winston Churchill

At this point, let's assume you're excited about great leadership and ready to learn about ways of practicing it. Before we embark on this journey, I invite you to consider a question: *for the sake of what* do you want to practice great leadership? In other words, what is the purpose behind your leadership?

I ask this question for both philosophical and practical reasons. Philosophically, if leaders are going to get better at leading, I prefer that they do so to achieve something larger than themselves, to promote the greater good. Practically, having a sense of purpose makes it dramatically more likely that you will both start and persevere in practicing great leadership. It provides an ignition for everything you do.

The practices I describe will challenge you and support you in becoming a better version of yourself. This involves ending old habits and starting new ones and, in turn, stepping into parts of yourself that you have intuited, but never fully trusted. As a new version of yourself is born, an older version gradually dies or at least shrinks in importance. As you read these words, you may be feeling excitement, fear, or both. One thing I can guarantee is that taking on new practices will be messy, uncomfortable, and confusing.

So why bother?

Seriously, why bother investing all the energy to make a shift in yourself? Why bother taking the risk of speaking and listening in new ways, of mending troubled relationships, of improving your posture and physical energy?

In my experience, one key factor differentiates managers who carry this hard work to completion from others who barely get out of the starting blocks: a sense of purpose beyond their own narrow self-interest. Getting a raise or promotion is great, but neither provides enough fuel to sustain the practice of great leadership. The source of such fuel is what the French call a *raison d'etre*, or reason for being: something you are trying to create, renew, rejuvenate, or replenish. This could be bringing to market a marvelous new technology, like a scalable substitute for fossil fuels. It could be teaching young women in the developing world to read. Or it could be building an organization where people feel safe and at home.

Without such a purpose, everything I'm going to suggest in this book will feel like drudgery—at best! With such a purpose, the hard work of practicing great leadership feels like a smart investment, one with risks, of course, but also the possibility of a positive return.

Discovering your sense of purpose isn't the easiest thing in the world to do. You may choose to avoid the question entirely, and for good reason: inquiring into your purpose makes you aware of how out of alignment your actions are with it. Conversely, if you don't know your purpose, there is little risk of feeling shame at being out of alignment with it! Contrary to myth, ostriches don't actually bury their heads in the sand. (Although they do lower their beaks down there several times a day to turn their eggs.) When predators show up, they run away. Why shouldn't managers do the same?

Zoological humor aside, what's it like to ask yourself about your purpose? If this exploration is uncomfortable but not treacherous, I encourage you to continue it by asking yourself a few questions:

- What do you want to be known for?

- What are your unique strengths and how do they intersect with what your organization, community, or world need right now?

- What do you feel passionate about taking a stand on?

- What does the world want from you?

- What would you risk embarrassment or fear to bring into being?

- Who would you be if you weren't held back by the past, but instead were pulled by the future?

As you explore these questions, you may notice that your purpose is not one thing but many things, and these many things are not always consistent. You may also find that there are actually levels of purpose within you, some more inclusive than others. I encourage you to call out these differences by sorting your potential purposes into a set of descriptive categories. In particular, start by naming the purposes that involve standing up for yourself and then expand outward from there.

This notion of expanding outward is captured by the concept of moral development. Psychologist Lawrence Kohlberg named the stages of moral development; his colleague Carol Gilligan updated them to accurately measure women, whose morality grows through "ethics of care" rather than "ethics of justice."[25] Ken Wilber renamed the stages "spans of moral concern" or simply "moral spans." Whatever terminology you use, the idea is that the wider your moral span, the greater the number of people and interests you consider when making decisions.

To distinguish your purposes, I suggest placing each potential purpose in one of the following categories. Each category represents a distinct moral span and carries specific implications for your leadership:

Me Leadership: You work and practice for the sake of your own achievement, happiness, health, and well being. Your concern is yourself and everything needed to keep you safe, secure, and content. This level of purpose may seem less noble than the two levels that follow, but it's not. In fact, it is foundational both practically and developmentally. On a practical level, if you can't define what's good for you, what business do you have advocating for what's good for others? From a developmental perspective, researchers tell us that humans need to develop a healthy egocentrism (*Me*) before it is possible to foster a healthy ethnocentrism (*Us*) or world-centrism (*All of Us*). This is why toddlers don't actually understand the meaning of sharing, teenagers struggle with fitting in, and most adults don't truly identify with a purpose beyond their family or organization until they are in their 40s and 50s.

Us Leadership: Your purpose—indeed, your entire sense of self— expands to include your team, your organization, your family, your tribe, your country, and so on. This is a major step forward. It means you exist for something larger than yourself. This is not better or worse than Me Leadership, just more inclusive. And it comes in both healthy forms (rooting for your favorite sports team, celebrating your religion's holidays, eating Thanksgiving dinner with your family) and unhealthy forms (picking a fight with the soccer referee who gives your daughter a yellow card, denouncing people of other faiths, and killing turkeys for the sport of it rather than to eat).

All of Us Leadership: In *The Needs of Strangers,* Canadian writer Michael Ignatieff asks, "What do we owe strangers?" It's a fascinating question because everything in our lives is touched by people we will never see or know. If you were to care as much about all people, including those who don't look or sound or live like you, as you care about yourself or those who are more similar to you, what would the expression of that care be? In asking this, I want to distinguish outer actions from inner purposes. When I was 18 years old, I participated in a Take Back the Night March on my university's campus. This looked noble and was, at least in the sense that the purpose was to declare the rights of women to feel safe after dark. But if you had excavated my mind, you would have found that I participated mostly to feel good about myself, distinguish myself from other men, and possibly even attract a woman from down the hall whom I fancied and who invited me to participate. From where I sit today, I would call that a clear Me motivation. So, as you start to distinguish different levels of purpose for yourself, please be mindful of All of Us appearances masking Me intentions. There is nothing to be ashamed of. We all do it. But be honest and put these purposes into the Me Leadership category.

I hope you find this exercise to be illuminating. I have. Working through it brought me to my current purpose: to develop great leaders in clean technology and sustainability. Currently, such leaders represent a small portion of my clientele. This could be a reason to feel embarrassed. Or it could be a reason to feel energized, have more conversations, and build relationships with new organizations. Which interpretation do you recommend I choose?

And, while we are on the topic, what is your purpose?

CHAPTER 7
FOCUS ON TWO THINGS

"I ALWAYS WANTED to be somebody, but now I realize I should have been more specific."
—Lily Tomlin

In the next two sections, you will learn about 15 practices—eight outer and seven inner—of great leadership. I encourage you to think of these as being on a menu, not an agenda. Your success as a leader and your happiness as a person don't depend on doing all 15 practices. In fact, if you try to do all 15, expect disappointment, if not distress.

My advice is to pick two practices—one outer and one inner—and give them your full attention. Here's why:

- Focusing your attention will give you better results than dispersing it widely.

- Selecting the highest leverage practices will give you benefits across many domains of your life. This assumes that you deliberately practice them, which is the subject of Part Four.

Despite this advice, you may find yourself so excited by the range of practices that you want to take up many of them. On the other hand, you may feel so overwhelmed by the amount of "work" that you feel like throwing the whole thing out. In either case, keep your mind tuned into this question: *What's the one thing that has the greatest potential to improve my leadership?*

Pick it. Practice it.

Practice it some more

THE OUTER PRACTICES

CHAPTER 8
HOLDING CONVERSATIONS FOR POSSIBILITY

"AS I STARTED [in 1985] to discuss the possibility of getting out of the memory chip business with some of my associates, I had a hard time getting the words out of my mouth without equivocation. It was just too difficult a thing to say."[26]

—Andy Grove

An amazing amount of work happens through conversation. Name any significant thing you've done in your life, and I bet you couldn't have done it without talking with someone about something. Right?

Yet we have this bizarre distinction between "talk" and "action." It's really an unfortunate use of words. I prefer to speak about different kinds of talk, some more action-oriented than others. One type of talk, *conversation for possibility*, is a crucial practice for great leadership. At heart this is extraordinarily simple: have a "what if" conversation about the future. Pick something that you and others might enjoy doing and discuss what it would be like, how it might look, sound, and feel, and what benefits might come from the experience. Don't ask what could go wrong. Ask what could go right. Don't get hooked on how somebody tried it in the past. Focus on how you might do it in the future. Most importantly, listen for what is possible, and if you don't hear anything, ask others if they do.

A PERSONAL EXPERIENCE

To give you a richer sense of conversations for possibility, this is the story of how I first learned about them:

Thirteen years ago in the lobby of a hotel in San Francisco's Union Square, a senior manager at HP was coaching me on how to get a girlfriend. I had just moved across the country from Michigan and was trying to make a few life changes. One was to get into a good relationship. My coach and I sat across a small round table, and I told her the story of my dating life: what I was looking for, how I approached things, who I had been dating, and how things tended to turn out. The full story, which I had never told anyone before, took two hours. She listened attentively the entire time. When I was done, my coach asked, "So, Amiel, I can see how important a relationship is to you and all the effort you've put into dating. What do you think is getting in the way?"

"I, um, really don't know."

"Let me give you my take." She drew a picture of three concentric circles—labeled, from the inside out, *Relationship*, *Possibility*, and *Action*. "There are three types of conversations. Each one has a purpose and is important in dating and the rest of life. A conversation for relationship is about exploring interests, finding out what the other person likes and doesn't like, so you have a sense of whether this is someone you'd want to spend more time with. A conversation for possibility is about *what if*. You pick something that interests both of you and talk about what it would be like to do that—say, visiting the zoo, hiking in the forest, or going to a concert. A conversation for action is where you actually invite her out onto a date—it's the first time you actually make a request or offer."

"OK," I said. "That makes sense. What's the problem?"

"I think you're jumping too quickly into conversations for action and skipping over the other two types of conversation. As a result, you're asking women out before you've gotten to know them and before they've gotten to know you."

In other words, bold action is great, but not without discernment. Conversations for action are necessary, but may fall flat without the presence of relationship and a sense of possibility.

Although I hated to admit it, she had a point. Once I found a woman attractive, I tended to plunge right in and ask her out. This led to one of two things happening. Either she said "no," and I felt disappointed. Or she said "yes," and I ended up going out with someone who was pretty, but not particularly interesting to be with. Either scenario made a sustained relationship unlikely.

My coach's insights were so on the mark that I decided to heed Buckminster Fuller's saying that if you don't act on a new idea in the first 15 minutes, it will never happen. That evening, at a party, I made a point while talking with women to listen for shared interests rather than just following the call of attraction. In a couple cases, I found myself bored or at least not enthused and excused myself. In one case, when I observed a great deal of common interests, I switched into a conversation for possibility. The details escape my memory, but it was something like, "So, I just had this image of us going out for sushi. Humor me for a minute: if we did that, what do you imagine you'd order?" I'm sure I was awkward—beginners always are—but it was a first attempt at exploring possibility before going into action. I ended up asking her out.[27]

In subsequent weeks and months, I made a point of paying attention to what kind of conversation I was having—not only in dating, but in all domains of life. I watched for two things:

- How much time I was spending in each type of conversation. Was I overdoing it on conversations for action? Or, in my quest to practice, did the pendulum swing too far toward conversations for relationship or possibility?

- How well I was sequencing the conversations. Did I first use relationship, then possibility, then action?

Over time, I found that I got better and better at this. My competence at conversation increased from mediocre to adequate. And it showed. I started enjoying the experience of dating more and found a greater sense of flow in work and friendships. Life was not perfect by any means, but it was the beginning of an important journey.

CONVERSATIONS FOR POSSIBILITY IN ORGANIZATIONS

After several years of practicing this myself, I began to introduce it to my organizational clients. In one case, a colleague and I led the senior management team of a large startup factory through an unusual exercise. We had people seated at tables of six. Our assignment for each group was to have a conversation about where to have lunch. There was a catch: two people were supposed to talk about what mattered to them in picking a restaurant (ambience, type of food, service, etc); two were told to describe what it would be like to go to one particular restaurant they liked; and the other two were instructed to propose specific places at specific times.

The intent of the exercise was to see how groups experienced having three very different types of conversations at the same time. The consistent result was confusion and frustration. One person would ask, "How about we meet at Joe's Bar and Grill at 12:30?" Another would answer, "I'm really looking for a place that will get us in and out quickly." And the third would say, "What if we were to find a place with an outdoor patio?" Three completely different conversations!

The amazing part wasn't that there was so much confusion and misunderstanding, but that it was so familiar to everyone. This bizarre way of talking around each other (without anyone naming it as such) operated much of the time, and it was costing them time and energy. In addition, in the push for fast decisions, the conversations for relationship and possibility typically got the short end of the stick, so the people initiating them gave up and went along with the pure action orientation.

What alternative did we introduce to this group? The very practice I suggest for you: start having more conversations for possibility. When you do, make sure that they are about topics that interest all participants. This requires knowing what people care about, which, in turn, depends upon astute observation coupled with prior conversations for relationship.

In other words, if you want to have better action and more trust, start by having conversations for relationship and possibility. This is so simple, but if your organizational culture has never encouraged it, it may not come easily to you.

MORE AND BETTER CONVERSATIONS FOR RELATIONSHIP

My advice for having better conversations for relationship is to keep things very simple. Start by doing them one-on-one over coffee or lunch—or spontaneously when you can grab someone for a few minutes. An ideal length of time is 30–60 minutes, but sometimes 5–10 minutes will do just fine.

If having one-on-one meetings is part of your organization's culture, great. If not, this may feel a bit riskier to you, so frame the invitation like this, "I'm working on X project and know you're working on Y. I think we may be able to help each other and I'd like to have a two-way chat to explore where our interests may overlap. Would you be up for a 30-minute coffee in the next few weeks?"

Now here are a few tips for having the conversation itself:

1. *Start briefly with context.* "Thanks for agreeing to meet. I'd like to ask you some questions about Y and would be happy to talk about X. Let's see where our interests overlap."

2. Ask a few simple, open-ended questions:
   - Can you tell me more about Y?
   - What are you hoping to achieve?
   - How are things looking right now?

3. *Listen very specifically for what the other person cares about.* Make a note of it in your mind—or include it in your meeting notes.

4. Ask follow-up questions:
   - What makes that important to you?
   - What was that like for you?
   - What do you like most about____?
   - What do you like least about____?
   - Could you say more about that?
   - Could you help me understand what you meant when you said____?

5. *Briefly summarize* the interests you have heard and ask, "Have I heard you correctly?"

6. *Be prepared to talk* about what you're working on and what makes it important to you. This is a good time to be real and err on the side of disclosing more than you ordinarily might.

When I ask leaders to hold conversations for relationship, the typical response I hear afterward is, "I got a much better understanding of where she's coming from than I ever have before."

This, of course, is the point: to get to know others' perspectives and interests so we can consider what possibilities we might explore with them.

MORE AND BETTER CONVERSATIONS FOR POSSIBILITY

That brings us to the main focus of this chapter: how to have more and better conversations for possibility.

The quantity of such conversations depends upon three main factors:

1. *Your mood.* If you're moping around in a mood of resignation or stomping around in a mood of resentment, your orientation will be to avoid conversations for possibility. It won't occur to you to initiate them and if others do, you'll steer clear.

2. *Your understanding of what others care about.* How well do you understand the interests and concerns of the people you work with? The more you know, the more ideas you'll have for conversations for possibility.

3. Your willingness to show up.

Once you agree to show up, you can increase the odds of the conversation being of high quality by doing the following:

1. *Pick a topic that involves shared interests* of the people involved or invite people who share an interest. It has to be something everyone cares about—not equally, but at least above a certain threshold of concern.

2. *Call it a "conversation for possibility."* This is not a time to be fuzzy. As we saw with the lunch decision exercise, weird things happen when people don't know what kind of conversation they are in.

3. *Remind everyone of the ground rules.* Do talk about the future, do talk about the good that can come, and do piggyback on others' ideas. Don't offer critiques (save these for later).

4. *Close the laptops* to avoid distractions. Use a white board or sticky notes to track ideas.

5. *Create a "parking lot"* for requests, offers, and anything that is outside of the conversation for possibility, including tough questions and critiques. Often the best parking lot is the one you maintain yourself. For example, if you're in the discussion and you have an idea that doesn't fit the ground rules, write it down. I know this sounds heretical, but you really don't have to say everything you think the moment it enters your mind. What you need is a trusted place to put it so you have confidence it will reenter your view later.

6. *Say "Wouldn't it be nice if…"* This phrase is a great way to introduce a possibility without advocating for it or making a commitment to it.

As I said, the hardest part of this may be getting started, simply because it's so unusual in your organization's culture. Once you get the ideas and imaginations flowing, you may be surprised what positive results ensue with relatively little effort. It may not look pretty or go flawlessly. The group will get off topic. People's critical minds will intervene. Someone's laptop will spontaneously open, and their fingers will mysteriously start typing. But this is all part of learning something new together, of building a new collective habit.

CHAPTER 9
TURNING TOWARD OTHERS

"THE BASIC PRINCIPLE that regulates how relationships work and also determines a great deal about how conflict between people can be regulated…has to do with the way people, in mundane moments in everyday life, make attempts at emotional communication, and how others around them respond, or fail to respond, to these attempts."[28]
—John Gottman, *The Relationship Cure*

A conversation for possibility creates a safe space for possibility thinking. That's great, but what about the fifty other conversations you have? How do you create space for great leadership there?

One way is to pay attention to *how* you interact with others no matter what you are talking about. Every day you have dozens of conversations ranging in length from a 30-second chat in the hall to a 2-hour meeting. Each conversation includes a multitude of subtle back-and-forth exchanges between you and others. The relational quality of these exchanges—how specifically you choose to respond to each other—has a substantial impact on your emotions and those of others. I refer to such exchanges as *micro-interactions*. They happen so quickly and habitually that you often don't notice them and can't describe them afterwards if asked. Yet, on emotional and gut levels, micro-interactions register in a big way.

Have you ever noticed that some people give you positive vibes when you are around them even when you are disagreeing vehemently, whereas others consistently rub you the wrong way even on seemingly uncontroversial topics? As I'll discuss later, this discrepancy may reflect your listening filter, the specific way you interpret your experiences. Or, if it turns out that many others experience similar reactions to these two individuals, the difference may be in the two of them more than in you.

To understand this difference in a way that allows you to bring a mood of possibility into your micro-interactions, let's turn to John Gottman, Emeritus Professor of Psychology at the University of Washington. Gottman earned fame as the person who can watch a newlywed couple interact briefly behind a one-way mirror and then predict with 90 percent accuracy whether they will still be married in five years. His predictions are based on very careful observation of the micro-interactions that happen between couples when discussing everyday topics. He has found that a small set of behaviors, like showing contempt toward your partner or withdrawing from connection, are highly correlated with divorce, whereas other behaviors, like gently supporting each other, are correlated with a stable marriage.

If this sounds obvious to you—*be nice, don't be mean*—I agree. The real value in Gottman's work, and the one that applies equally well to leadership, is that he distinguishes three ways you can *turn* when somebody else reaches out to you within a conversation. Gottman calls this reaching out a "bid for connection." Bids can be large ("Would you like this job?") or small ("Can you hand me the marker?"), subtle ("I was impressed with that speech") or direct ("I want you to give that speech at all seven sites"). In all of these cases, Gottman's research suggests that the person receiving the bid has three choices for responding: turn toward the other person, turn away from them, or turn against them.

Consider this simple example: You're walking in the parking lot before work and bump into a former colleague. The two of you worked closely on a project until she left for another team. You tell her that the old team is getting together over lunch in two weeks to celebrate the success of the project and "it would be great if you could make it." You've made a bid for connection. Your colleague can respond in one of three ways:

- She can *turn toward* you. "Yes, that sounds great, I'm there. Thanks for inviting me." But what if she cannot make it? She can still turn toward you by saying, "Bummer, I'll be out of the country then, but otherwise I'd love to come. Is there any flexibility in the date? If not, can I join you all some other time?"

- She can *turn away* from you by ignoring you ("Sorry, gotta run"), changing the topic without acknowledging your question ("Whatever happened to Smithy?"), or physically turning her body in a different direction.

- She can *turn against* you. The cold approach: "Nope, I've moved on. Not interested." The critical approach: "So, you guys actually made it. I never would have expected that given the caliber of the team." Or a tone of contempt: "Are you serious? Don't you remember *anything* of what things were like?"

One bid for connection. Three very different responses. As you imagine yourself on the receiving end of each response, what is your experience like? How does it feel to be with this person? Are you more or less likely to make a future bid for connection with her?

Gottman found that the three responses have dramatically different effects on relationships. Turning toward produces more bidding and responding and causes relationships to grow. Turning away and turning against both reduce the amount of future bidding. But whereas turning away increases conflict by producing hurt feelings and causes relationships to end relatively quickly, turning against leads to conflict-avoidance by suppressing feelings and causes relationships to end more slowly.[29]

Gottman's research team also found that when one person makes repeated bids for connection and the other consistently turns away from or against them—which he calls "unrequited turning"—the relationship heads south quickly:

> Once bidders are ignored or rejected, they usually give up trying to connect in the same way again…People seem to lose heart…Among people in stable marriages, spouses re-bid just 20 percent of the time. In marriages that are headed for divorce, people hardly re-bid at all. Instead they simple fade away from conversations, relinquishing their attempts to connect.

Do these research findings sound familiar to you? They sure match my experience, both professionally and personally. Several examples come to mind:

- Several years ago, I had the opportunity to see in action an executive who was expert at turning toward others. He is known in his company as one of its most promising leaders, someone who could run a Fortune 500 company in the next decade. On the one hand, he does many of the things other hard-nosed leaders in his company do—set high expectations, hold people accountable, and ask challenging questions. On the other hand, he does these things in a way that others enjoy being around him. He has this effect because he consistently turns toward others even while disagreeing with them. I once heard a conversation in which he was angry and willing to show it, yet there was still the sense that he was turning toward people involved in the situation.

This is not easy to do! Consequently, even in the midst of strong disagreement, the collective mood around him was positive.

- Not long ago I coached a different executive who was a pro at turning against others' bids for connection. No matter what others would say, he would respond with some version of "No." Sometimes it was a gentle, "No, that's not going to work." Sometimes it was a more hard-edged criticism or insult. Even when he liked what the other person was saying, he would start out by pointing out where he disagreed. I remember talking with him once after a meeting where I had observed this happen literally thirty times with the same person, whose energy level had dropped more and more with each iteration. I said to my client, "You sure did turn against her a lot." His response: "No, actually I really respect her a lot. I just want to make sure she is thinking things through. There's so much that can go wrong." Turning against others' bids can become so habitual that it affects every exchange. It took quite a bit of practice, reflection, and feedback for this executive to shift his responses to everyday situations.

- I have an acquaintance who is extraordinarily gifted at turning away from people. No matter what you say to him, he ignores you, changes the topic, or simply stares off into the abyss. He has a successful career and by most measures is a mature adult, yet in the most routine interactions about the most basic things, he cannot help but turn away. I've offered feedback and even described the impact on me, but I've come to the conclusion it's a lost cause. Why do I share this example? Because if great leadership includes the practice of turning toward others, it also includes the practice of not getting entangled in continuing to bid for connection with people who cannot or will not turn toward you. As we'll see in the chapter on "neutralizing enemies," it may still be useful to develop a neutral and respectful relationship with this person, but not to extend yourself beyond the response you are receiving.

- I'm currently involved in a project with a small team of people who are skilled both individually and as a team at turning toward. It's not that they do anything big or momentous. It's more how they respond to all the little things that comprise a project: asking for information via email, requesting a reschedule for a meeting, talking about a draft report, appreciating hard work, passing a napkin across the table at lunch, and so on. I have a sense, even when we see things very differently, that they trust and respect me. This is not something I imagine or remember from four years ago, but it's something that now gets renewed and reinforced with each micro-interaction.

This "turning" stuff is a big deal, and it comes down to an extremely simple idea: the way you respond in a microsecond to another person's bid for connection, when multiplied over hundreds of interactions, constitutes your relationship with them. It *is* your relationship with them.

Try on this concept for a moment, and I think you'll find that the implications are momentous. If you want to build an organization of people who are highly engaged and filled with a mood of possibility, one of the most effective things you can do is to start turning toward people—not just once, but continuously as a regular practice. Consider that in an average 60-minute meeting, you have anywhere from 5 to 50 opportunities to turn toward others. How many of these opportunities will you seize? In the same meeting you have a similar number of temptations to turn away from or against others. How many of these will you succumb to?

The bad news is that this takes effort. You can't just interact with people. You have to observe yourself interacting with them.

The good news is that the slightest shift, when repeated hundreds of times, can elevate your leadership substantially. Attend to the small stuff, over and over again, and you'll produce some really positive big stuff.

CHAPTER 10
FLIPPING COMPLAINTS TO COMMITMENTS

"BEHIND EVERY COMPLAINT is an idea or belief or a value that a person is committed to. Otherwise why be upset? A person who complains that his boss is a jerk might be committed to the idea of having a relationship with a boss that is based on respect and trust."[30]

—Lisa Lahey, co-author, *Immunity to Change*

I'm big into flipping things. Burgers, eggs, omelets—and words. (Notice I didn't say "middle fingers"—that's in the other guy's book.) Flipping words means more than just saying something different. It's a literal substitution. You take something you are about to say and replace it with something else because the new words reflect the better version of you.

This happened to me in a powerful way when I was in my late 20s. One day over lunch a friend pointed out to me how often I used the words *should* and *need to*. This was less a criticism than a "something you may not have noticed." In fact, I had not noticed it. The words *should* and *need to* were to me what water is to fish: something I swam in 24/7. How could I be aware of something that was always in my experience? I couldn't.

My friend's advice ended at what not to say. For an idea of what to say instead, I turned to a book. Sadly, I don't remember the title or the author, but I can tell you what it said: stop talking about what you should do and start talking about what you want to do. This meant using words such as *I'd like* and *I want* and *It would be great if* and *I've decided*. The author made it sound like switching to these words was as easy as putting on a new pair of shoes. Hardly. Admitting that I wanted something was foreign to a mind accustomed to following rules of how to act. Declaring that something would be great violated an inner commitment to not get my hopes up because things could come crashing down. So flipping words wasn't easy. But I did it, and gradually my language shifted. Having a cue—hearing myself about to say the word *should*—proved to be a great help. As a result, these days the word *should* is rarely heard coming from my lips, and I don't think you'll find it many times in this book. (If you do, you really should not tell me).

I share this story for two reasons. First, it demonstrated for me the challenge and power of flipping words. Second, the act of trying this myself opened me to the idea of using the "flip" approach to handle a more pervasive organizational pastime: grumbling, moaning, and complaining.

Complaining. We all do it. We all listen to others do it. And sometimes we even complain about it. (Can you say *viral?*) In fact, we even have a word that makes complaining sound productive: *venting*. It's such a fine metaphor:

Tanya: Hey, Bob, sounds like you need to vent.
Bob: Yep. Time to open up that gable vent and air out my emotions.
Tanya: And not a moment too soon. It was getting stuffy in there.

Venting is prevalent in most organizations and particularly pervasive in paranoid cultures. When there is a mix of fear and distrust, there is a lot to complain about! Venting is like eating or going to the bathroom: something everyone needs to do to get through the day. Actually, most people are more likely to skip lunch than miss an opportunity to complain. (Go ahead, track this yourself for a week). Some erroneously call it a sign of emotional intelligence and compassionate listening. But that's just rationalizing something that drains the life out of organizations by sucking people into negative moods.

So what do you do when you hear someone else start to complain? This is the million-dollar question. The most common response to complaining is to listen to it, encourage it, and/or add your own tales of woe. The assumption is that this creates camaraderie, but it's camaraderie of the miserable. To use Gottman's terminology, it's *turning toward*, but turning toward negativity.[31]

Another common response is to *turn against* complaint in an attempt to shut it out and shut them up. "Suck it up," you say. "Haven't you said enough about that?" Or, half-jokingly, "Dude, you're bringing me down." (I don't know the female version of Dude, but the same principle applies). All of these potential responses reduce trust and send the complainer off in search of friendlier ears.

Finally, there is *turning away*. When someone complains, you ignore them or change the topic. Or, once you've identified someone as a perpetual complainer (sometimes known as an "energy vampire"), you simply avoid interacting with them. In truly extreme cases, this may be an appropriate response. From a managerial perspective, what do you do when an energy vampire has claimed victims for years without remorse? Either give employees garlic to carry around (hey, it's less expensive than a "mental health" sick day) or find another place for the energy vampire to hang out. Seriously, the only thing worse than an energy vampire employee is an energy vampire manager running performance reviews that involve ranking employees. But we've already nailed that coffin shut, haven't we?

Is there a fourth option, one that sustains mutual trust without creating a caravan of woe? I learned from Robert Kegan and Lisa Lahey[32] that there is. It's called flipping complaints into commitments. The basic idea is that behind every complaint is something you are committed to. If you watch your complaint closely, you'll get a pretty good idea of what you care about.

For example, one senior manager I coached was continuously frustrated with others not following through on their promises. People would promise to do something and then not do it. He brought this up with me constantly. Rather than let him gripe forever or tell him to shut up, I asked him to consider what was behind this complaint. After a moment of reflection, he identified it: a commitment to reliability.

I encouraged him to say this out loud: "I am committed to reliability." Although reluctant at first, he finally got the words out of his mouth. "How did that feel?" I asked. "Awkward," he replied." "Great," I said. "Try it five more times."

He was silent. I realized that my request wasn't clear. "Please try it out five times *now*." "Oh," he replied, and then repeated this declaration five times out loud. As I listened, I sensed that he was getting more comfortable with each iteration. After the last one, I asked him, "So, how was that." He thought for a minute and said, "It's alright. Not bad. I can actually feel this is something I mean. I really am committed to people being reliable."

The entire practice session I just described took less than five minutes. For this manager, the practice presented quite a challenge, no less than the one I experienced in flipping *I should* to *I want*. Fortunately, it was the beginning of a sustained practice. Over several months, he found that every time he acknowledged his commitment to reliability, whether out loud to others or quietly to himself, it energized him. It brought him in touch with what he was moving toward, a space of possibility. This fired him up.

When it comes to flipping complaints to commitments, two points bear repeating. First, it's a great way to shift your mood and create a space of possibility around you. Second, you can't just do it once and expect results. As with every other practice, competence grows through repetition. Going from mediocre to decent to good takes hundreds of repetitions. Going from there to great takes even more.

So how can you start flipping complaints to commitments? I suggest these steps:

1. *Pay attention* to what you're complaining about. A coworker? Your boss? A direct report who seems out to get you? How dreadfully slowly things change in your organization—or how painfully fast? Whatever it is, write it down.

2. Take a few deep breaths and notice: *where is this complaint occupying space in your body?* Where are your muscles tight or pained? Breathe into these areas so you can relax and feel more prepared for the next step.

3. Ask yourself *what do you care about so much* that its absence from your experience is causing you to complain? What are you committed to? Trusting relationships with coworkers? Clear expectations with your boss? Thoughtful change? Whatever it is, write it down. Make sure you start the sentence with, "I am committed to_____." The words matter because they immediately position you not as a victim who complains but as a powerful person who has commitments.

4. *Say it out loud* to a trusted colleague or friend when an opportunity presents itself. (If it's something you're truly committed to, pay attention and there will be boundless opportunities.) It will feel awkward, but so what? That just means you're a beginner. With practice it will get easier. If you're doubtful about this, skip ahead to the chapter on Visualizing and incorporate your new

commitment into the exercise of imagining possibility so that it becomes a reality within you.

5. Over time, *notice when your declaration spontaneously comes out of you.* Pay attention to what that feels like to you and how it impacts others. Appreciate how much less effort it takes today compared to a month ago. Imagine what it might be like to build your conversations around this commitment in the future.

Remember: you may have been raised to complain, but you were born to flip.

CHAPTER 11
ARGUING BETTER

"ANY TIME FOUR New Yorkers get into a cab together without arguing, a bank robbery has just taken place."
—Johnny Carson

A surprisingly large percentage of managerial missteps—like ignoring market signals or failing to execute on commitments—are due to mediocre arguing. Arguing, my term for the candid and respectful airing of perspectives, is one of the best ways to test your assumptions, fill in your blind spots, and expand your perspective. Sometimes you'll hear people say, "C'mon folks, stop arguing." Maybe it's my New York roots, but I am very comfortable with arguing. My only beef with arguing is that we don't do it well enough.

While working in North Carolina in the mid 1990s, I saw many examples of people avoiding or stifling their own inclination to argue. They kept their differences to themselves to be polite and remain cordial—at least on the surface. In Oregon, we run a version of this called "Northwest Nice." In both cases, the candid airing of perspectives is missing. It's mediocre arguing by omission.

Then there is mediocre arguing by commission. This occurs in organizations that encourage debate but do it poorly. In the case of paranoid cultures, they do it very poorly. The problem isn't too little airing of opinion but too little learning; not too much deference but too much vehemence; not hidden decisions but poorly grounded decisions; not too much light, but too much heat.

The recipe for mediocre arguing looks something like this:

1. Gather a bunch of strong-willed people together.
2. Give them something to talk about.
3. Provide them with 10-15 years of role modeling the following behaviors: advocating for your own position, preparing your next position while the other person is speaking, and listening only for what you find disagreeable, risky or otherwise suspect.
4. Discourage the use of white boards or flip charts for documenting and clarifying ideas.
5. Schedule their days tightly so they're looking at their laptops half of the time in order to catch up on work.
6. Make the laptop work engaging enough that they aren't too distracted by the discussion but not so engaging that they miss hearing points they find objectionable.
7. If at all possible, promote and reward these people based on individual performance, preferably by ranking them against each other. Even better if the person doing the ranking is in the room.
8. Bake for 90 minutes in a cramped room, preferably with no natural light.

Yes, I know what you're thinking. For a book about possibility, this is a dark and even cynical vision. But that's the point, isn't it? If paranoid organizations weren't so de-energizing and their arguing so mediocre, there would be no need for great leadership.

As it turns out, mediocre arguing is a potent force in keeping organizations from realizing their potential. It produces lots of noise but little that is audible; lots of heat but little light. More specifically, the lack of learning between people lowers the quality of decision making. The vehemence of advocacy pushes people apart. And the atmosphere of suspicion and distrust makes it harder to evoke people's best, keep them engaged, and retain top talent.

Great leadership calls for very different behaviors and structures around arguing. Some of these involve systemic change that is beyond the scope of this book. But a significant portion of these behaviors is very much in your hands.

Before you use these hands to increase the quality of arguing, I want to disabuse you of a popular notion. Some managers think that productive conversations—the kinds that promote learning and mutual understanding—require you to be *nice* or *soft* or *lose your edge*. This is item #57 on my list of leadership straw men. Although it provides a convenient excuse to keep doing things the same old way, it's an assessment with little grounding. Think about the people you know who can simultaneously describe their perspectives with clarity and power *and* encourage others to do the same, who can hash through disagreements with respect and patience. Would you call these people *weak*?

I don't use the term weak to describe human beings (unless referring to their physical capacities), but if I did, I certainly wouldn't use it to describe someone powerful enough to have a tough, candid, and respectful airing of differences. That just doesn't make sense. In fact, two of the mostly highly regarded corporate CEOs of the past few decades, Jack Welch and Lou Gerstner, were frank and hard-nosed men who were passionate about having vigorous and respectful debate. Both had flaws—we all do—but that didn't stop them from arguing well.

So if you can assume for the moment that learning to argue better is an act of power, then what might you do to increase the quality of your arguing? Here are five suggestions:

1. *Don't confuse assessments with assertions.* People waste enormous amounts of time because they don't know the difference between these two "speech acts." Any time you hear an argument about who's right and who's wrong, you are seeing this confusion in action. So let's get this clear. Assertions are statements of fact that can either be true or false. Assessments are statements about the quality of something that can be either grounded or ungrounded. *It's 70 degrees outside* is an assertion. You can verify it by looking at a thermometer or weather.com. *It's hot outside* is an assessment. It cannot be true or false because assessments can never be true or false. You can provide evidence to ground your assessment that it's hot, but there is no way to be right. (*Everyone in our group says it's hot outside* is an assertion. You can verify it by asking people.) A huge proportion of arguing in organizations is about whether or not it's true that it's hot outside. People's emotions and identities get wrapped up in being right about something that is not objectively verifiable. What's the alternative? When you are describing your view, call it "my take" or "my assessment." When you are summarizing someone else's, call it "your take" or "your assessment."

2. *Ground your assessments.* Using words like "take" and "assessment" is an important first step. It can lift a conversation out of miserable confusion and into a space of possibility. The next step is to describe the rationale or data behind your assessments. "Let me tell you why I think it's time to exit this market." "I can think of three solid reasons why Julie would be a better hire for this role than John." These explanations of "the why" are as important as they are rare, particularly in the middle of heated discussion. They are important because they allow you to test

your assumptions and help others understand why you see things the way you do. They're rare in heated arguing because they involve reason, and the reptile brain that gets activated at such moments is by definition not reasonable. (Ever met a reasonable alligator?) Even when you're not emotionally triggered, grounding assessments can seem both difficult and risky—difficult because you haven't actually thought through your reasoning; and risky because revealing your assumptions allows others to challenge them. The good news? Grounding your assessments makes you simultaneously more persuasive and more trustworthy.

3. *Invite others to ground their assessments.* When someone tells you their perspective, it's tempting to immediately reply by advocating for your own, perhaps even interrupting them in the process. Stop doing this. Seriously, your default response isn't helping you, the other person, or the conversation. Instead, invite your colleague to ground her assessment. "Madhu, it sounds like your assessment is that it's time to exit this market. I'm sure you've put a lot of thought into this. Could you please walk me through your reasoning." Or, "I know you discussed this assessment a few months ago but a lot has changed since then. Could you help me understand your thinking behind this today?" By the way, the phrase *help me understand* is an absolute gold mine. It positions you as—and transforms you into—someone trying to learn rather than someone trying to critique.

4. *Make it visual.* For over twenty years I've been using flip charts, white boards, and sticky notes to facilitate conversations. These simple tools work because they give groups a "public memory" of what's been said. They're visual, and visual learning works. It amazes me how many teams ignore such tools or use them poorly. In most cases, people are simply following the habits of their cultures. In some cases, that means "leading by PowerPoint," which is as effective as exercising by watching TV.

In other cases, that means relying on people's ears to have superpowers that make visual learning unnecessary. Either way, the cultural habits are so entrenched that it takes courage to walk up to the white board and start capturing ideas. Fortunately, such actions yield real dividends. When you see your ideas—particularly your assessments and the rationale behind them—on a white board, you're more likely to "feel heard." When others see those ideas, they are more likely to understand your thinking and create genuine questions to ask. Then you can have a healthy and vigorous argument.

5. *Put peripheral topics in the "parking lot."* It's hard enough to have one good conversation at any given time, much less several. That's why when peripheral topics emerge, I suggest you put them in the "parking lot," ideally, on a white board or flip chart. This keeps the group focused on the topic at hand and allows the person who brings up the "peripheral" idea to have confidence that the group will return to their topic later.

In summary, a big part of leadership is arguing. Great leadership is about arguing better.

CHAPTER 12
TELLING POWERFUL STORIES

"A STORY NOT only expresses motivation, it motivates. It not only describes learning, it embodies, reflects and causes learning. Telling the story over and over makes it real. As the group's story evolves and grows, it becomes a vehicle through which the group can act 'as if' and bring new ideas and worlds into being."[33]

—Lisa Marshall, *Speak The Truth and Point to Hope*

Storytelling has always been a core part of leadership. But only recently have the people who study, teach, and coach leadership begun to talk about it.

What do we know about telling stories that is relevant to great leadership? Let me summarize what I've learned:

1. Stories can be incredibly powerful because of how they affect the human brain, and they comprise a large part of people's everyday conversations.
2. All managers tell stories, but their stories vary widely in quality and relevance.
3. Good stories share a common structure. They have protagonists, challenges, conflicts, and resolutions. They have beginnings, middles, and ends. Sometimes they have villains.
4. Good leadership stories consciously include listeners as protagonists. Everyone feels like an actor in the story.
5. Great leadership stories connect people's everyday experiences to the strategic challenges of the organization.
6. Great leadership stories also evoke positive emotion and inspire people to take action.
7. Great leadership storytelling requires more than just a great story. Other essential elements include the physical presence (voice, facial expressions, body posture, and movement) of the storyteller and use of visuals, location, and timing.
8. Great leadership storytelling isn't the only way to express a story. The other option is to embody it.

Embodying a story of great leadership is what I teach best. It's what this book is about. If you're interested in learning more about how to *construct and tell* great leadership stories, consider these resources:

*   Nancy Duarte's book *Resonate: Present Visual Stories that Transform Audiences*. Duarte introduces a powerful methodology for giving persuasive presentations. My favorite part is her recommendation that speakers invite audiences into a tension between "what is" and "what could be"—not once but multiple times in a talk.

*   Howard Gardner's book *Leading Minds: An Anatomy of Leadership*. Famous for his theory of multiple intelligences, Gardner writes about several prominent leaders in business, government, and

academia whose success derives in large part from the stories they communicate and embody. Gardner claims that the most effective stories are those that appeal to the "unschooled" (6-year-old) mind that thinks in terms of right and wrong.

- A TED Talk by Hans Rosling called "New Insights on Poverty." Rosling is a genius at bringing numbers to life with flair and amazing visuals. He is an answer to the question: how do you tell a great story with data?

- Stephen Few's books *Show Me the Numbers: Designing Tables and Graphs to Enlighten* and *Information Dashboard Design*. Once you've read Few, you'll be embarrassed by the quality of charts in your organization, learn to instantly recognize "chart junk," and become way more adept at telling stories with numbers.

- *Beyond Bullet Points: Using Microsoft Office PowerPoint 2007 to Create Presentations that Inform, Motivate, and Inspire* by Cliff Atkinson. Detailed tips on planning your slides, creating storyboards, adding graphics, and delivering your presentation. The author also happens to be a friend and a man of great emotional depth.

- *Three Stories Leaders Tell* by Chris Cavanaugh-Simmons. This book by a highly regarded Silicon Valley executive coach shows how to construct three types of leadership stories: "Who am I?" "Who are We" and "Where are We Going?"

- *For All Time: A Complete Guide to Writing Your Family History* by Charles Kempthorne. How do you mine your life for stories that could be useful to your organization? This book is a great guide.

If you had to choose between telling great stories and embodying a great story, I'd encourage you to select the latter. However, if you have the inclination to improve at both, these resources are a great place to start.

Chapter 13
Listening Like a Master

"PEOPLE NEED THE ability to listen very openly to other people. Most of us tend to listen with a bias to what we already know and value."[34]

—Carol Weber, Darden School of Business, University of Virginia

The first five outer practices for great leadership all involve listening. Now it's time to hone in on what it takes to listen like a master. This is the first time I've used the word *master* in this book. This is deliberate. My intent is to emphasize how important it is to listen with extraordinary skill, because if you can do this, you can do everything else. Listening like a master allows you to see possibilities where others see problems, know when and how to turn toward others, appreciate the commitments behind people's complaints, understand divergent perspectives, make grounded assessments, construct powerful stories, and appreciate what makes others tick. These abilities, in turn, help you make better decisions, build better teams, retain top talent, and foster cultures of trust and possibility. If you listen like a master and others around you do, too, the paranoid qualities of your organization's culture will melt away as quickly as ice cubes in a pot of boiling water.

These are bold statements, wouldn't you say? After all, isn't listening a "soft," unimportant skill not worthy of academic research, much less the valuable time of practicing managers? Aren't you already a good enough listener? And even if you wanted to become a better listener, how much can you really do to change things? These are all important questions, so I'll handle them in sequence.

What Makes Listening So Important?

It is true that the amount of research on listening in organizations is scant. This is due partly to its reputation as a "soft" skill and partly to the logistical difficulty of measuring listening quality. My own belief in listening as a pivotal leadership practice stems largely from two sources: my experience helping leaders listen more skillfully and my efforts to become a better listener myself. In both cases, I've seen anecdotal (if not rigorous statistical) evidence that listening pays big time.

Let's begin with a personal example. When I was 22 years old and in my first adult job, the company that hired me was a national consulting and training firm led by a handful of seasoned and very talented consultants. I was the junior guy trying hard but in way over my head. Salient fact: the man who preceded me in the position left it to direct the training function for a mid-sized American city. In contrast, I was still trying to figure out how to function without professors and grades.

Perhaps the hardest part of the job was responding to my boss's requests and feedback. At the time, I thought he was overly demanding and critical. In retrospect, I realize that I was listening to him through a powerful filter that went like this: does he trust me, or doesn't he trust me? No matter what he did or said, my mind and body interpreted it as a response to this question. Because he set high standards and was not shy about letting me know when I didn't meet them, my reactions to him were often negative and defensive. In phone conversations, I froze, my body unable to tolerate the difficult physical sensations from the perceived attack. In written correspondence, a medium with which I was historically more comfortable, I concocted long and elaborate arguments in favor of my positions coupled with emotional pleas for him to take it easier on me. The Ice Man by phone and the Criminal Defense Lawyer by email and fax. That was how I listened, so that was how I rolled.

I could have maintained this listening filter for the ensuing twenty years. It's unlikely I would have become an executive coach, but I could have done many other things reasonably well. Not admirably and not happily, but at a level of adequacy that would pay the bills.

Fortunately, this is not what happened. When I was in my early 30s, I became aware of this listening filter and the pervasive impact it had in my life. To be clear, I call this realization "fortunate," but it was far from pleasant. Who wants to discover that a huge percentage of his experience is driven by a preoccupation with whether or not others trust him? Not me. That's not who I took myself to be. In fact, it was a bit like you would feel if you learned that you've had bad breath for a decade and never knew about it: ashamed at how you'd been and embarrassed that you were oblivious to it.

The fortunate part is what happened next. I found a teacher, James Flaherty,[35] who showed me what was happening and taught me to approach this matter with compassion, not criticism. I found friends who were willing to put up with my shenanigans and support me in reducing their number and severity. And I started to practice new ways of listening.

To make a long story short, I spent three years rigorously observing the pervasiveness and impact of my trust/distrust listening filter; three years imagining what it would be like to own, rather than be owned by, this filter; five years practicing conscious self-correction whenever the filter interfered with my listening; and two years experiencing the filter less as an enemy and more as that crazy relative that shows up once a year at the holidays with strange gifts and stranger jokes.

The result of all this effort? Not just higher quality listening, but a more frequent experience of ease, confidence, and inner strength.

But enough about me.

Let's turn now to an organizational example, one based on composites of real people I've coached:

You are a Senior Vice President in a Fortune 500 company. Two middle managers are giving a presentation to you about dramatic shifts in the industry. They describe these shifts as major threats to the company's core line of products and suggest new strategic directions. Now, you may not know it consciously, but you are wired to listen to this presentation through a particular filter. Like all filters, it allows certain information to go through and blocks off the rest. Your filter works as follows: will this make me look strong or weak? So, as you listen, this is 75 percent of what you are paying attention to even though it's less than 1 percent of what's actually happening.

If you're unaware of this filter, it owns you. You shut these managers' insights out of your awareness because taking them seriously is an admission of weakness. After all, would a strong executive need a bunch of middle managers to tell him what's happening in the industry?

On the other hand, let's say you are aware of your listening filter. At the very moment you start to disregard the managers' perspective, you catch yourself listening through the strength/weakness filter. "Oh, there I go again," you think to yourself. This moment of awareness allows you to listen deeply to the presentation and appreciate the substance behind it. This does not mean you believe everything you hear or accept the presenters' recommendations as given. It means you are strikingly more likely to take what you hear seriously and integrate it into your own thinking. Instead of being owned by your listening filter, you own the filter. Ironically, freeing yourself from the strength/weakness dichotomy makes you a stronger leader.

That's you. Now let's introduce Sasha. She is one of the middle managers preparing to present to you. As she meets with her colleague to outline the presentation, she starts to get anxious. As the colleague walks through the signals of industry transformation, Sasha's mind imagines all the ways her presentation will fail if she actually describes these: You will lash out at her angrily—or quietly seethe in a way that gets the same message across. She will feel humiliated. Her own manager will get angry. She will be fired or, at best, demoted. These thoughts filter how she listens as she prepares for the conversation.

Now, here's the point around which everything else pivots: is Sasha aware of this listening filter? If not, she does everything she can to prevent these dangers. Rather than framing her insights in a way you will understand, she tries to take these insights out of the presentation entirely.

On the other hand, let's say Sasha is aware of her listening filter. She catches herself imagining worst-case scenarios and self-corrects. She realizes those scenarios are assessments, not the truth. She looks for evidence that alternative assessments may come true. And she is more likely to give you the powerful presentation you need to hear.

What's going on in this story? The ability of two leaders to have a constructive conversation that moves the company's strategy forward depends largely on whether these leaders recognize what keeps them from fully listening. If either you or Sasha is unaware of your listening filter, the company will miss a great opportunity to reconsider its place in the market. If Sasha goes soft on the presentation, then you won't learn about her insights, much less benefit from them. If Sasha tells it as she sees it but you filter out the vital message, you'll leave that meeting thinking you know everything you need to know—a blind spot, to say the least. Given your influence on other senior leaders, the company may miss the boat strategically. Given the weight of your power in Sasha's experience, she may decide to never again take such a risk. Who knows how much time will pass before a similar opportunity arises?

On the other hand, if both you and Sasha are aware of your listening filters, things will unfold in a dramatically different fashion. The exchange between you will be focused and fruitful. You, Sasha, and the company will gain.

AREN'T YOU ALREADY A GOOD ENOUGH LISTENER?

Thinking that you are already a good enough listener rests on two premises:

1. Being a good listener is sufficient. There is no need to shoot for mastery.
2. You are already a good listener.

Let's tackle the sufficiency assumption first. Part of me agrees with this statement. In a world of mediocre listening—even the best intended of us have strong filters that block out relevant insights—isn't good listening good enough?

Well, good enough for what? For good leadership? For moderately competent leadership? Well, yes, of course it is. But I don't think that's what you're shooting for.

Now, onto the second premise. For sake of argument, let's assume that being a good listener is sufficient. Do you believe you are a good listener? If so, what evidence can you present to ground this assessment? As it turns out, research by Cornell University suggests that most managers overestimate their own listening skills.[36] If you think you're great, you're likely good. If you think you're good, you're likely decent or mediocre. Listening is one of those skills whose quality becomes apparent only when truly put to the test. It's just like humor and singing. You think you're funny because whenever you tell a joke, your mother thinks it's hilarious and your ten-year-old kid laughs hysterically. Then you say the same thing in a meeting at work and you get nothing. Try it at open mike night at the comedy club and you'll be walking home with bananas smeared on your shirt. As for singing, unless you have a great voice, you will *always* sound better in the shower than at the karaoke party. Being skilled at listening works the same way.

HOW MUCH CAN YOU TRULY IMPROVE YOUR LISTENING?

You can improve your listening a great deal under two conditions:

1. You're willing to deliberately practice over a substantial period of time.
2. Your practice includes not just mechanics of listening, but also working on the heart of what gets in the way of your listening.

By this point in the book, you've figured out that I am fond of deliberate practice, so let's talk about *what* to practice to achieve listening mastery. In the story about Sasha delivering a presentation to you, what mattered most was your awareness of your listening filter. As it turns out, you'll find very little about listening filters in most books and classes about listening. What you'll find is a great deal on the mechanics of listening: where to look at someone (just above the nose), how to hold your head (slightly to the side and occasionally nodding), and what sounds to make ("Hmmm," "Yes," and "I see").

There's nothing wrong with these tips. I use them myself. But they provide only a small part of the guidance you need to achieve listening mastery. What they leave out is a response to—or even an acknowledgment of—the most vital question about listening: what gets in the way of good listening?

As we've already seen, everyone listens *for* certain things and screens out the rest. Even if two people hear the same thing, they interpret what they hear differently based upon what they are listening for. These people may share the same physical world, but they carry in their minds very different worlds of interpretation—different world views. There's nothing wrong with listening through a filter—it's how our brains have been wired. What matters is whether or not we are aware of this filter.

What are the specific things you listen for? What are all the other things that this filter screens out?

This is likely new territory for you, so let me provide a simple map. For the sake of this exploration, assume that there are nine listening filters—nine broad patterns of what people screen in and screen out of their attention. Each person, including you, has access to most of these filters some of the time but tends to use a single filter disproportionately more of the time. When you discover yours, think of it as your "home base" or "center of gravity" filter.[37]

Here are the nine filters:

- Am I being criticized? Am I right or wrong about this?
- Am I being appreciated for the help I've given?
- Am I getting credit for my achievements? Or could this negatively affect others' impression of me?
- Does this person see how unique I am?
- Is this going to drain my energy and resources?
- Am I being distrusted? What could go wrong here?
- Is this situation exciting or boring? How can I plan for more fun?
- Who is in charge here? Who is weak and needs my protection?
- Is there harmony here or conflict?

I share this list not so you can identify your filter—that takes more investigation—but to display the wide range of filters that different people have. I hope this encourages you to do the work it takes to discover your "home base" filter so you can develop a deeper awareness of it and reduce its power over you. (I'll discuss ways to identify your filter in the chapter on "healing your Achilles' Heel.")

Once you identify your primary listening filter, the next step is to do a few simple things a large number of times:

1. *Observe the presence of your listening filter* in your experience—all the ways it shows up (physically, emotionally, cognitively) and the impact this has on you and others.

2. *Start to question* the necessity of having this listening filter dominate your experience at all times and in all situations. Are there occasions when perhaps it is less necessary?

3. *Experiment with naming* your listening filter when you become aware of it and noticing how this affects your response to situations.

4. As your listening filter becomes an object in your awareness, practice *putting yourself in other people's shoes* as you are listening to them. Feel the sounds enter your ears. Sense the movement of your breath enter your lungs. Feel yourself connected to them, perhaps by imagining a chord of light connecting your heart to theirs. (This last one is a bona fide Jedi Mind Trick. It will give you superhuman powers of understanding.)

Here's to listening like a master.

CHAPTER 14
ASKING GREAT QUESTIONS

"LEARNING IS NOT compulsory. Neither is survival."
—W. Edwards Deming

Throughout the previous chapters, I've emphasized the importance of questions, both the ones you ask yourself and the ones you ask others. Now let's put this topic front and center.

I want to start by assuming that you're sold on the value of asking great questions. Fair enough?

Excellent. Now we can explore what constitutes a great question and how to incorporate more great questions into your conversational repertoire.

My initial exposure to asking great questions came during that first job out of college that I discussed in the last chapter. My company consulted to organizations in health care and higher education. I was given responsibility for behind-the-scenes work like conducting phone interviews and summarizing data. Sensing my anxiety about interviewing medical school faculty and administrators, my boss gave me the following advice: "Ask a lot of dumb questions. You'll learn more. If you're afraid that this will make you seem dumb, then tell people you're going to ask them a lot of dumb questions." When I asked him what he meant by "dumb," he said "open-ended." So that is what I did, and it worked well. Not once did one of my 50-year-old interviewees say, "Hey, kid, what do you think you're doing interviewing me?" On the contrary, the humbler (and crisper) my questions, the richer the responses they gave me.

This experience taught me three lessons. First, the most powerful questions are often about obvious things that, until now, nobody has had the curiosity or temerity to ask. Second, people like to be asked open-ended questions and given a *lot* of time to respond. Interrupting is bad. Keeping your mouth shut during awkward silences is good. Finally, even a nervous and inexperienced kid can ask great questions, so if you either have experience or lack nerves, there's no excuse for not raising your game.

In the twenty years since I started that first job, I've conducted more formal interviews than I can recall. Asking powerful questions has ceased to be a conscious practice and is now an unconscious habit. That's not to say I don't ask weak and ineffective questions from time to time. I do. But constructing and asking solid questions is now a core part of my identity and one of a few things for which people consistently acknowledge me (sometimes to say "Amiel, cut it out with all the questions!")

Let's talk about what constitutes a great question—or, more specifically, what constitutes asking a great question, since the question itself is only part of the package. As with listening, learning the mechanics of constructing and asking questions is necessary but not sufficient. Equally important are underlying factors like the intention and mood behind your question. In the remaining part of this chapter, I'll share what I've learned about the content of questions and the intention and mood we bring to asking them.

THE CONTENT OF A QUESTION

I used to spend a lot of time thinking about what questions to ask someone. Then I discovered that constructing questions can be relatively simple. The trick is to identify a small set of phrases that are consistently effective at evoking thoughtful responses from others and then use them as often as possible. I think of these as *power phrases* because when incorporated into questions, they elicit powerful responses.

Below are my favorite power phrases, categorized based upon the three types of conversations introduced earlier: conversations for relationship, conversations for possibility, and requests, a core part of conversations for action.

CONVERSATIONS FOR RELATIONSHIP

In conversations for relationships, success is understanding what matters to the other person and helping them understand what matters to you.

- What did you like best about____?
- What did you like least about___?
- What was that like for you?
- Can you help me understand____?
- Can you tell me more about____?
- What's your take on_____?
- What makes this important to you?
- What would____ [success, happiness, an ideal job, a fun evening on the town, etc.] look like to you?
- If you had to change one thing about____, what would you change?
- If I were to ask you_____, what would you say?

The first time I consciously used some of these questions outside of work was in 1994. I found myself living in a six-bedroom house in Chapel Hill, North Carolina with only one other housemate. He was the chief tenant and therefore responsible for selecting other people to join us. Worried about who he might pick, I offered to run the housemate interview process. My goal was to get to know applicants' habits and preferences without first revealing what I was looking for. This would prevent them from selling me on what they thought I wanted. I held eight or nine interviews for four spots, and each one became a conversation for relationship. Here is what I asked:

- What are you looking for in a house?
- What are you looking for in terms of housemates?
- When you've had housemates in the past, what has worked well for you? What has not?
- If you were to name one thing that would make you want to move out of a house because it was so unpleasant, what would that be?
- If I were to ask your past housemates to describe you, what three adjectives would they use?

It was amazing to observe how much people revealed about themselves and how greatly this helped us in assessing them for fit. Granted, some people's actual preferences likely differed from their stated preferences, but for the most part, their answers were predictive of their behaviors. In the end, all four housemates we selected ended up being excellent fits.

CONVERSATIONS FOR POSSIBILITY

In conversations for possibility, success entails exploring a possible future scenario or decision *without critique* in order to experience what that future may be like and what benefits it can bring. For example, you could ask:

- What if we were to___? What might that look and sound like?
- If we were to_____, what positive results would you expect to see? What new possibilities would open up?
- Assume for a moment that____were possible. What conditions would need to be present for it to work?
- Who else might be interested in this? What would they be excited about?
- What if we were to combine____with____—how might that play out?

REQUESTS (A PART OF CONVERSATIONS FOR ACTION)

In requests, success involves speaking to a specific person (rather than to an amorphous group), establishing clear conditions for satisfaction (exactly what the other person needs to do for you to feel satisfied), setting a specific timeframe, embodying a mood of possibility (as opposed to resentment or resignation), conveying that *Yes* is not the only acceptable response (also acceptable: *No*, a counteroffer, or a promise to get back to you later), and actually speaking the request (as opposed to just thinking it).

It takes a lot to make a good request! That's why the question you ask as part of the request is so important. As you read the list of questions below, please keep in mind that the most effective phrasing depends entirely on the situation: what are you requesting? Who are you asking (and what's the power relationship between you)? How interested do you think they'll be in fulfilling the request? Is this something that they'll see as a chore, or something they'll actually enjoy doing? How important and urgent is this request to you? The specifics of the situation will dictate the best way to phrase the question.

- Will you_____?
- Will you agree to_____?
- Would you be willing to_____?
- Would you like to_____?
- Would you be interested in_____?
- Do you have any objection to_____?
- Will this work for you?
- What will it take to make this work for you?
- If I_____, would you be willing to_____?

Disclosure: my number one favorite phrase for making requests is *Would you be willing to_____?* This conveys respect by implying that the other person has the will—and freedom—to accept or decline. It also avoids the trap of pointing to what the other person likes or wants. You're not asking *Would you like to do this?* You're asking *Would you be willing to do this?* Finally, this phrase works in a wide variety of situations with a broad range of people. Such multiplicity of use comes in handy when you want to practice asking questions and have the mental bandwidth for only one approach. You want to pick the one you can use everywhere, right?

THE MOOD AND INTENTION BEHIND A QUESTION

Ten years ago, I gave a workshop to a group of fellow executive coaches about how to avoid "conversational breakdowns." I talked primarily about which words were effective and which words might get you into trouble. The group enjoyed the distinctions I made and seemed animated by the topic. Then my friend, Steve March, raised his hand and politely said, "Amiel, what you're saying about language seems very important. However, I wonder how effective any of this will be without the right intention." The comment caught me by surprise, not because it was a new concept, but because it was one I had accidentally omitted from the workshop *despite how important I knew it to be.* At that moment, I made a commitment to myself that whenever speaking or writing about language, I would always talk about the mood and intention behind the words.

Thank you, Steve.

Now, let's assume you've become highly competent at constructing questions. What difference does the mood and intention behind your question make?

MOOD

Let's start with mood, the emotional field in which you regularly live. Mood is to emotion as climate is to weather. In the context of asking questions, your mood influences both you—the energy and integrity you bring to the question—and the other person—the emotional space they experience while hearing your question. For example, consider three different moods you can have while making a request:

In the first case, you walk up to someone in a mood of resentment. Your face is angry, and your breath is shallow. You're not a happy camper. When you reach out to them to make a request, what happens? Odds are good that the other person will think, "She sure has a chip on her shoulder. Not sure I want to get involved in that."

In the second case, you approach that same person in a mood of resignation. Your shoulders sag, and your voice is flat. When you make the very same request using exactly the same words, what happens now? It's likely that the other person will feel your flat affect and low energy in their body. Even if they like you and want to help, they'll feel little inspiration to sign on.

In the third case, you approach that individual in a mood of possibility. Your face, voice, and body all convey strength and excitement. Now you make the exact same request. Do you expect the person to respond differently than in the first two cases? Undoubtedly yes, because your physical and emotional energy evokes something positive in them.

Mood has a similar impact on conversations for relationship and possibility. The emotional space you create either opens or closes the space of possibility between you and the other person.

INTENTION

How does intention differ from mood? Your intention is the specific outcome you want from asking a question. More often than not, your intention lives below your field of awareness. You think you're asking a question, but in reality you are playing another game with its own peculiar goals and rules. What sorts of games do people play while asking questions? I've played all of these games myself, so here are some examples from my own experience:

- When I was 23 years old, I met with my boss for my first-ever performance review. After telling me how much he enjoyed my work, he asked, "So, Amiel, do you want to make a case for how much you want to be paid, or do you want me to tell you how much you will be paid?" The question confused me, but I interpreted it literally and proceeded to argue for a particular salary increase. My boss was frustrated by my response. An uncomfortable 40-minute argument followed. Later I realized that my boss's intention wasn't to hear my preference about salary, but to communicate that he had already made a decision.

- When I was 29, I had coffee with a semi-famous leadership consultant who knew everybody. He was a generation older than me. Going into the meeting, I told him, "I'm not looking for connections. I just want to talk with you." During the meeting, I asked him a series of questions about his work. In theory, it was a conversation for relationship. In reality, what I really wanted was for him to introduce me to people he knew. He eventually figured this out and called me on it. I felt ashamed.

- During a phone conversation, a close relative interrupted me multiple times without apology. I got angry. "You continue to interrupt me," I said, "and I'm getting very frustrated. What's it going to take for you to stop?" I didn't care about his response and didn't want to hear it. I wanted to drill home how angry I was while appearing reasonable and mature.

- My wife had been out of town for a week. I'd been home with the kids. The night before she flew back, I asked her, "How would you say this trip has been for you?" I cared about her answer, but I already knew she'd had a great time. What I secretly hoped was that she'd thank me (again!) for holding down the fort. This was exactly what she did.

In each of these examples, the person asking the question is up to something. They don't say it, wouldn't admit it if asked, and may not even be aware of it. But it's right there below the surface, and the other person feels it. In none of these cases is the person's intention to learn from the other person or even invite an authentic response. Instead, curiosity is trumped by fear, manipulation, anger, or resentment.

Hopefully, these examples give you a sense of the range of intentions that can lay behind any question. Here is a back-of-envelope model called *Amiel's Ratings of Intentions Behind Questions:*

- A: Asked with curiosity and openness to having your own assumptions overturned
- A-: Asked with curiosity and the hope that your assumptions will be confirmed
- B: Asked to get an objective response
- C: Intended to gently point out defects or steer in a direction
- D: Intended to badger, criticize or force in a particular direction
- F: Intended to humiliate or cause other forms of damage

CHAPTER 15
MAKING PEACE WITH ENEMIES

"IF YOU BELIEVE breaking is possible, believe fixing is possible."
—Rabbi Nachman of Breslov

How healthy are your relationships with the people most pivotal to your work? What would healthier look like, and how can you take your relationships there?

Many people don't ask these questions. Leaders in fear-based organizations never ask these questions, because what's the point? Their relationships are what they are. They're not going to change, and if they do they'll get worse, not better. As people often say to me, "Charles and I can't stand each other, and we will never be best friends, so what's the point?"

At first this sounds reasonable. Charles likely will never be your best friend. But, it has all the signs and flaws of classic straw man argument.

What you're really saying is this: if a lousy relationship cannot suddenly morph into a great friendship, then why bother improving it?

As though mediocrity and perfection were the only two options.

When you put it that way, the whole argument sounds ridiculous, yet literally millions of people use it every day to avoid improving relationships. The cost is substantial: toxic relationships that don't improve remain toxic. They drain more time and energy from organizations than just about anything else. And, to repeat the key point, they don't need to be great to be better than toxic. Very often, a neutral and respectful relationship will do just fine.

Making peace with enemies means investing the time to improve the lousy relationships until they're at least neutral and respectful. And, while you're at it, to improve the other relationships that truly matter. Let's walk through the steps for doing this.

WHICH RELATIONSHIPS ARE IMPORTANT?

To start, make a list of the relationships that are obviously important to you: your boss, your direct reports, your peers, and any internal or external customers. Now add to this list the names of people who have helped you make something happen in the past, those who could block what you're doing, and those who "own" key resources or have the ear of the people who do. We'll call these your important relationships.

WHAT IS THE CURRENT QUALITY OF THESE RELATIONSHIPS?

Here comes the fun part. For each person on the list, make an assessment of the health of your relationship. Use the following scale:

1. *Toxic*—neither of you can be in the room with the other without feeling ill.

2. *Negative*—when you're around each other, it isn't relaxing and can feel unpleasant.
3. *Neutral/Respectful*—no warm fuzzies but also no ill will.
4. *Positive*—you enjoy each other and have a mutual respect.
5. *Great Vibe*—being around each other is easy and effortless. Your conversations "flow" and fill you with positive energy.

WHICH RELATIONSHIPS ARE TRULY PIVOTAL?

Now it's time to focus. If you were to pick three to five relationships to invest in improving over the next six months, which ones would you choose? I suggest you use a single criterion for making this decision:

Which relationships, if improved, will have the greatest positive impact on your ability to accomplish your goals and fulfill your purpose?

Notice that I'm not asking you to assess the value of a relationship. I'm asking you to assess the value of the improvement in a relationship. The ones that rate most highly are your pivotal relationships.

WHAT DOES AN IMPROVED RELATIONSHIP LOOK LIKE?

Take a look at this list of three to five pivotal relationships. Ask yourself, how healthy would you like each relationship to be in 6 months? What would an improvement in each look like? There are two rules to remember when thinking about this:

1. The relationship improves at least one point on the quality scale.
2. Every relationship ends up at least at Neutral/Respectful.

WHAT CAN YOU DO TO IMPROVE THE RELATIONSHIP?

The specific steps you take to improve each relationship depend upon many factors: the current and desired future health of the relationship, your strengths and style of building relationship, the other person's preferred communication style and medium, the intensity of your current work together, the nature of your working relationship (peers, boss, direct support, etc.), and the specific history you have with each other. Nonetheless, there is a handful of practices worth considering regardless of your particular situation:

1. *Apologize.* Have you done anything in the past that hurt the other person? Have you ever apologized for it? A simple apology given with sincerity and heart can go a long way.

2. *Say thanks.* Keep an eye open for little things the person does that you appreciate. These could be things they've done for years that you've never noticed or acknowledged. Thank them for these actions. Be sure to mention precisely what it is you appreciate and the specific positive impact it has on you.

3. *Have a conversation for relationship.* Schedule time to find out what's important to the other person and reveal what you care about. Speak genuinely and listen openly. If you already know that they like Thai food, suggest having this conversation over lunch at a Thai restaurant.

4. *Turn toward* them. Every micro-interaction you have with them is an opportunity to make small improvements in your relationship by turning toward them.

5. *Stop doing something* that bothers them. Everyone has pet peeves, so this person likely has one related to you. Find out what it is and stop doing it.

6. *Acknowledge changes* they've made. If you've started to change how you interact with this other person, it's quite possible they will change how they behave toward you. When they do something positive, however small, appreciate it. Don't contrast it to what they used to do but simply acknowledge their effort and the positive result.

If you take these steps and adapt them to your situation, you can neutralize your enemies and strengthen your ties with your friends.

This is a good time to review the eight outer practices of great leadership and ask yourself, which of these could have the biggest impact on my leadership? Remember that I'm encouraging you to select one outer practice and focus on it like a laser beam.

The next step is to get familiar with the seven *inner* practices of great leadership. What can you do when nobody else is looking to increase your capacity to lead others into a space of possibility? This question brings us to Part Three.

PART THREE
THE INNER PRACTICES

CHAPTER 16
VISUALIZING

"THE WORLD BELONGS to those who cross many bridges in their imagination before others see even a single bridge."
—Chinese proverb

In the 1988 World Series, Kirk Gibson hit one of the most memorable home runs of all time. With two outs in the bottom of the ninth inning and the Los Angeles Dodgers trailing 4-3, Gibson pinch hit a game-winning homer. What is remarkable is that he did it with two injured legs—the man could barely walk—against one of the top relievers in the game, Dennis Eckersley, and only after fouling off multiple pitches with the count at two strikes. You've probably seen the famous video of him hobbling around the bases and pumping his fist into the air.

What you may not know is that right before Gibson hit that home run, he visualized it in his mind. Literally. He created a mental image of himself knocking the ball over the fence. And then he did it.

This visualization practice had been part of Gibson's repertoire for years. I first hear about it in 1984 when he played for my hometown team, the Detroit Tigers. In that World Series, he hit a game-clinching homer in the 8th inning, his second of the game, against another amazing relief pitcher, Goose Gossage. In an interview after the game, he talked about how he had visualized the homer while he was standing at the plate. I remember thinking to myself, "That's weird, but, wow, did it work!"

Just as it has in many other fields, including business. Visualizing success is a proven method for elevating performance. It operates by creating within you a scaffolding for what you will then create outside of you. Visualizing is part of preparing for performance. More importantly, it is a practice you repeat over and over again until it comes naturally to you. By the time Gibson hit his climactic homers in the 1984 and 1988 World Series, he had been visualizing them for years.

What experiences have you had visualizing positive possibilities? In what domains of your life have you used visualization? Sports? Academic performance? Giving a speech? Entering a difficult conversation?

I invite you to consider the impact that visualization can have on your leadership. Consider the outer practices of great leadership. How might visualization support you in taking on these practices and thereby elevating your game? Let's say you decide to have more conversations for possibility with your peers. What would it be like to quietly envision yourself having one? Can you picture it now? Or let's assume you want to argue better by getting really good at asking others to ground their assessments. Can you create a picture in your mind's eye of what it would feel like to do this and the impact it would have on the conversation?

As you dip your toe into these examples, you may be reminded of my earlier challenge to identify your purpose. In both cases, you are acting from a place of volition or conscious choice. However, there is an important difference. Your purpose is what you stand for now and forever. Visualization puts you in touch with a particular experience involving particular people at a specific point in time. For example, it is energizing to declare my current purpose, developing great leaders for clean technology and sustainability. However, this declaration conveys nothing of what my experience will be like in the future. Nor does it help me see myself having amazing conversations for possibility with the leaders I intend to serve. Both of these require acts of visualization.

So how do you do it? There are a number of effective methods. Popular ones include doing closed-eyed visualization, drawing pictures, and writing mock future news headlines describing in past tense what you've accomplished. I recommend trying them all to find what works best for you. First, try this simple exercise you can do right now in less than five minutes:

As you think about your current work, please fill in the blanks:

- Wouldn't it be nice if_____?
- Wouldn't it be cool if_____?
- Wouldn't it be great if_____?

I recently assigned this exercise to an executive I'm coaching who has a big job involving enormous complexity and pressure. In three minutes, he came up with five items, all of them things he would really love to see happen yet that he had not to that point articulated. What allowed him to do this? I'd love to say it was my presence, but I'd put my money on the framing of the sentence. There's something about *Wouldn't it be nice if* that frees up your energy and jump starts your imagination. If you're feeling resignation about what's possible, it lifts you up out of that. If you're feeling resentment toward people getting in your way, that, too, falls by the wayside. Better yet, there's no promise specified or implied by the statement. You are trying on the idea, not making a commitment to it. This evokes a positive mood. You feel lighter and more open. This is precisely what happened with the executive who did the exercise.

Unfortunately, not everyone follows the instructions. More than half of the people who try this exercise verbally skip the all-important initial phrase and simply fill in the blank.

Overheard recently at a conference room near you:

Amiel: "OK, Ralph. Tell me what you came up with."

Ralph: "The organization can get through this rough patch without losing anyone or laying anyone off."

Amiel: "Ralph, my good friend, you've accidentally left out the first part of the sentence, *Wouldn't it be nice if.*"

Ralph: "Oh, yeah, you're right. It did feel fragmented. Here goes again: Wouldn't it be nice if the organization could get through this rough patch without losing anyone or laying anyone off."

Amiel: "Now, what's that like to say?"

Ralph: "Better. More positive. More energy."

Amiel: "Great. Wouldn't it be nice if you could learn to do this all the time?"

Ralph: "Very clever, Amiel! But, to answer your question, yes, it would be very nice. It would be great."

I invite you to try this yourself. Pick one of the outer practices:

Wouldn't it be nice if_____?

CHAPTER 17
SEEING PATTERNS

"TO UNDERSTAND IS to perceive patterns."
—Isaiah Berlin

Now that you're learning to see future realities that exist within you, let's try something different. How about seeing past realities that exist outside of you? In particular, let's look for two kinds of patterns:

1. Patterns of behavior in your organization's interaction with the marketplace that reveal emergent organizational strategies.
2. Patterns that reveal your team's strengths.

The capacity to *see patterns* is an inner practice that can bolster great leadership in numerous ways. For example, identifying your organization's emergent strategies (which we will define shortly) gives you material for compelling stories and provides a useful foundation for constructing great questions. In a slightly different vein, understanding your team's strengths opens the door for conversations for possibility about what you can accomplish together by blending strengths. It also helps you argue better by knowing whose assessments to trust on which topics and how to best encourage them to ground their assessments.

ORGANIZATIONAL STRATEGIES

Most people think of a strategy as a ploy or plan for the future. And it certainly can be that. But a strategy can also be a pattern of past actions—not what was intended, but what resulted. Henry Mintzberg calls this an *emergent strategy*. "Strategies," he says, "form as well as are formulated. So even good ones need not necessarily be conscious and purposeful."[38]

A classic example of emergent strategy was Honda's entry into the United States motorcycle market. The Boston Consulting Group, in a case study used for years in MBA classes, described this as a deliberate market strategy conceived by Honda's senior executives in Japan. Most businesspeople believed this story because it matched the way they thought about strategy: as a plan for the future. Then Richard Pascale stepped in. When he interviewed the Honda managers who sold the first motorcycles in Los Angeles, a dramatically different story surfaced. Their assignment was to sell large motorcycles that company executives assumed would appeal to American consumers (because Americans "like big vehicles"). But this didn't work out as planned. What happened instead is that people in Los Angeles started calling Sears to request smaller Honda motorcycles that weren't even on sale in the United States. Why? Because they saw Honda salesmen driving around Los Angeles on these smaller vehicles. Over time, the sales managers caught onto what was happening—they noticed a pattern of behavior—and responded by placing orders for the smaller motorcycle. In Mintzberg's words, the company's strategy wasn't formulated. It formed.[39]

Another example of emergent strategy was Intel's decision to exit the memory business. There is a famous story about how, at a pivotal moment, Gordon Moore and Andy Grove conducted a thought experiment in which they fired themselves, physically left the room, came back in, and decided to stop manufacturing the DRAM (Dynamic Random Access Memory), which was Intel's bread-and-butter product. This story is true, and it presents a wonderful illustration of great leadership. Humility and courage meshed in a single moment, bringing a powerful question, great listening, a conversation for possibility, and two leaders turning toward one another.

Yet there is a story behind this story. You can find it described in Grove's book, *Only the Paranoid Survive,* and detailed in Robert Burgelman's book-length study of Intel, *Strategy is Destiny.* A few years before the famous thought experiment, Intel middle managers had started shifting production away from memory and toward other products like microprocessors. They had seen what Moore and Grove had not: the market and field of competition were shifting. As importantly, they were able to translate this heretical insight into action without senior management approval. Why? Because microprocessors produced higher margins than DRAM. They automatically received favorable treatment in decisions about manufacturing allocation.

Grove and Moore's thought experiment was therefore more than simply a deliberate strategy. It was also a ratification of a pattern of behavior that had occurred for years. It recognized an emergent strategy and gave it a large stamp of approval.

There are countless other examples of emergent strategy—Mintzberg's writings are full of them—yet the world of management continues to assume that strategy is always a plan you design rather than a pattern you discover. The reasons for this range from the cultural (deliberate strategies give us a sense of control and constancy) to the pedagogical (deliberate strategies are easier to study and explain) to the political (if strategies emerge, then who needs CEOs?) to the financial (without deliberate strategies to sell, how will blue chip consulting firms stay in business?). There is no getting around it: deliberate strategy is here to stay.

But let's give emergent strategy its rightful place. That means building the capacity within yourself and your organization to recognize patterns of behavior that just might, from the proper vantage point, reveal something significant: New customers and markets to capture; competition that is greater or less than you assumed; and businesses to enter, grow, diminish, or exit. Just consider the possibilities. In fact, you may even discover new ways of tapping into and combining the gifts of your people as their own strengths rise into view.

STRENGTHS OF PEOPLE

People surprise you. Just when you think you know who they are and what they are capable of, they do something completely unexpected. Like lead a seemingly unmanageable team, resolve an insurmountable human conflict, or shine in an area everyone "just knows" they are weak. This is the limitation of putting people in boxes as though they are inanimate objects. This is also the reason we speak about "human potential" and, in honest moments, acknowledge that each person's true potential is a mystery.

Fortunately, as a manager, there is something you can do: watch your team members very, very closely. Notice what activities are easy and effortless for them. Notice what allows them to enter a state of "flow," when they are so immersed in action that they lose track of space and time. Notice, too, what gets them out of bed in the morning and what keeps them up at night (which, if you watch closely, are different things). Notice how they behave around you versus how they behave around others. Notice what they're like in the morning as compared to the afternoon, what gets them emotionally triggered versus what relaxes them, and what they do when they don't know what to do.

When you observe like this and when you do it with care, you'll pick up on patterns. These patterns will inform the decisions you make, like what assignments to give them, which teammates to match them with, how to help them build their careers, and what it takes to keep them engaged, happy, and employed in your organization. These decisions, in turn, will shape the possibilities you create as a manager and the mood you evoke in the organization around you.

This ability to see patterns in people is a powerful gift. If your organization has solid practices for succession planning and leadership development, you can put that gift to use there. Because now you are a talent scout. Your job is to assess different people's performance and potential and to discern where to invest the organization's development resources—not training or coursework, but the time and attention of senior managers. Notice the patterns of behavior you see in people two and three levels below you in the organization. What challenges do they face in their on-the-job experiences? What are they learning from these experiences? When they move to different roles or assignments, how do they handle the transitions? What do new challenges reveal about their capacity to rise to the highest levels? And, to make things real, how does it feel when you are around them? Do you feel a sense of constraint and resignation, or are you energized by a feeling of possibility? Can you allow yourself to be emotionally affected by others even while you try to evoke positive emotions in them? Can you become part of the very pattern that you are seeing?

PATTERN RECOGNITION

The good stuff doesn't always come naturally, particularly when nobody has taught it to you. Discovering emergent strategies and recognizing strengths in people are both acts of pattern recognition. They involve not analysis, breaking a whole down into its parts, but synthesis, bringing the parts together into a whole. Almost nobody teaches synthesis—anywhere. If your schooling was like mine, you learned to analyze, not synthesize, and took pride in being "analytical." (My organic chemistry and macroeconomics textbooks didn't teach synthesis).

Instructors specialized in particular subjects—whether mathematics, French, mechanical engineering, or political science—and rarely strayed from them. In high school, I took a marvelous class that integrated American History and English (titled "Integrated"), but that was a big exception. Within any given class, when it came time to integrate all that you had learned during the year, was this an exciting moment of synthesizing the myriad lessons into a cohesive whole? Hardly. It was a time to stress out, eat poorly, sleep little, and hold your breath until it was over.

Most organizations don't do much better at teaching you to recognize patterns or synthesize. They're divided into departments or functions, each with its own language and rules. If you're an individual contributor and you propose something bold that connects your work to another function or department, you may get patted on the back, but it's equally likely that you will be discouraged from pursuing such a collaboration because it's "outside your scope." If, on the other hand, you're a first line manager, your scope is larger, but in most places you're still rewarded for the success of your team, rather than the success of the larger organization. As you rise to higher levels in the organization, you take on greater scopes of responsibility that require you to see and integrate more and more perspectives. To paraphrase educator Robert Kegan, every promotion brings new "mental demands," the challenge to handle ever greater complexity.

Challenge is essential to growth and, the research tells us, pivotal to leadership development. But it creates distress and disorientation rather than development when not joined by sufficient support. As the complexity in your job rises, who teaches you how to manage this complexity? Who models how to synthesize and make sense of all the perspectives that suddenly confront you? If you are among the fortunate few, your organization has a long tradition of helping managers learn how to stretch their minds to meet each successive growth in scope. That responsibility is owned by your current boss, who not only interacts with you regularly (unlike a mentor or external coach), but also has gone through that very leadership passage herself. She can teach you because she has lived it herself.

Wouldn't that be nice?

I ask the question because it's likely you're not one of the fortunate ones in this situation. Instead, you have to figure everything out for yourself. Your boss either hasn't gone through this leadership passage herself, doesn't have the skill to coach you through it, or simply lacks the time or incentive. She has her mind on other things, and what's the reward for developing people anyhow? If she exposes you to the people and assignments that would teach you what you cannot learn now, she might lose you to another division. There's no victory in that. As a result, the virtue of teaching you to see patterns and synthesize takes a back seat to the vice of hoarding talent. Actually, to call it a "vice" is misleading. Your boss is acting in integrity with what the organization expects.

It's a sad story, not just because the missed opportunity is so great, but because what is required to seize it is relatively simple. Seeing patterns is primarily a cognitive act. You do it with your brain. Yes, emotion can support or detract from synthesis. Yes, as we'll soon see, a relaxed and centered body helps. But the core act of synthesis is primarily cognitive. So in a world of managers who have spent years honing their cognitive abilities, this seems like the perfect thing for experienced managers to teach their direct reports. If I didn't know any better, I'd figure that the managerial ranks would be filled with capable synthesizers. But they're not.

Fortunately, as we've seen, every complaint points to a commitment. Once I recognize how much I value synthesizing and join with others who share this commitment, my disappointment morphs into resolve.

And so I ask the same of you. What would it be like to become really good at seeing patterns, say in the strengths of your team? What possibilities would this create for your team's work together? What greater influence would this allow you to have within your organization? Most importantly, what would it feel like to be the kind of leader who was a whiz at spotting others' strengths and knowing how to employ them to good ends?

CHAPTER 18
HEALING YOUR ACHILLES' HEEL

"YOU ARE NOT the water you swim in, only the water you drink."
—Sean Casey Leclaire

Don't let your Achilles' Heel become an Achilles' Hell.

If you're human, you have flaws. And there is probably one big one that can screw up your career or, at the very least, limit your potential for great leadership and/or big promotions. We call this the Achilles' Heel in homage to a mythical Greek warrior who was invulnerable in battle except for his foot. I describe the Achilles' Heel as a set of habits wired into your brain and body that limits your repertoire of leadership behaviors. In other words, it constrains your degrees of freedom. Fortunately, the latest neuroscience teaches us that these habits can be rewired even well into adulthood.[40] The leaders I work with accomplish this through deliberate practice and rigorous self-observation. This takes courage and focus, but the result is greater energy to respond to complex decisions and challenges.

How would you describe your Achilles' Heel?

Here's my hunch: you have a very good idea of the behaviors that get you into trouble. One or two dozen performance reviews have taught you that. But do you know what is behind these behaviors? Wouldn't it be nice to have a better understanding of the thought patterns and habitual emotional reactions that produce these behaviors so you can nip those habits in the bud?

No, not really, Amiel. That sounds unpleasant. Pass the beer nuts.

Let's assume you're willing to muster the courage to delve into these inner experiences. Let's say you are up for honing in on what makes you tick—and that you might actually appreciate what you get out of this. How might you learn about your Achilles Heel, and what would you do with the new understanding?

A BRIEF HISTORY OF THE ACHILLES' HEEL

Before we go there, I'd like to provide a very brief history of the Achilles' Heel concept in leadership. In the late 70s and early 80s, researchers at the Center for Creative Leadership (CCL) identified a set of leadership *derailers*. If you're a train speeding down a track (rather than a Greek warrior entering battle), these are the factors that can throw you off track. It was wonderful research, and it had several significant upshots. One was for organizations to take the time to identify leaders' derailers and then do something about them. At that point in time, leadership derailers generally weren't on organizations' radar. First, because the concept hadn't been invented and, second, because in the United States companies had experienced a remarkable period of growth without significant global competition since World War II. I don't think it's a coincidence that the CCL study happened shortly after the United

States stopped being the only economic game in town. A second upshot of the research was that certain organizations saw the value of going beyond the simple reward strategy of promoting managers up the chain. To teach managers the lessons they needed to lead on a larger level, CCL suggested employing lateral moves. For example, if you have an operations manager with solid results and great potential who is lousy at listening to others, put them in a customer service management role where the job itself forces them to practice listening.

As robust and practical as the CCL's research was, it had far less impact on managerial practice than the researchers had hoped.[41] First, the notion that leaders have a single big potential derailer was far outshined in the marketplace by the concept of competencies. When your organization asks you to do a 360, the result is a report that lists anywhere from fifteen to a hundred different competencies. A bunch are strengths. A bunch are weaknesses (or "development areas" or "opportunity areas"). This is all fine and good, but the sheer number of items detracts from the focus on a single Achilles' Heel. When I work with leaders who have received a 360, my first task is to help them find the signal in the midst of all this noise.

The other competition to the notion of Achilles' Heel is the growth of the strengths-based school of leadership development. If you've taken the StrengthsFinder instrument, you've been part of this school. Personally, I can't imagine coaching leaders without an understanding of their strengths. And I would agree that leveraging your strengths is a wonderful way to develop. Where the strengths-based school goes overboard, in my opinion, is in its insistence that people develop best in their area of greatest strength. This may be true for many first-line employees, but it is not for managers for the simple reason that the complexity and pressure of their roles is incompatible with an unattended Achilles' Heel. Someone gets hurt. So my take—grounded in research and my own experience—is that leaders develop best in *both* their area of greatest strength *and* their Achilles' Heel.

For strengths, my favorite instruments are StrengthsFinder 2.0, created by the Gallup Organization, and the VIA Survey of Character Strengths. The latter is available for free by registering on the University of Pennsylvania's Authentic Happiness web site. There are also many excellent books on this topic like *Now, Discover Your Strengths*, *Strengths-Based Leadership*, and *Go Put Your Strengths to Work*.

IDENTIFYING YOUR ACHILLES' HEEL

As for identifying your Achilles' Heel, there are a number of instruments and tools you can use. My favorite is one with an unusual name: the Enneagram. It's a model of nine personality types. Each type describes a deep and fundamental pattern of making sense of experience that drives what you pay attention to and what you ignore. Remember the listening filters from the last chapter? Each listening filter is an expression of a particular personality type. As we've seen, if you're not attentive to it, it can get you into all sorts of trouble. That's one reason I joke that the Enneagram describes nine potential paths to Achilles' Hell. Fortunately, the Enneagram also shows the nine roads to great leadership precisely by helping you get free from the constraints of your Achilles' Heel. Rather than putting you in a box, it shows you the box you put yourself in every day—and how to escape it.

The nine Enneagram types are known as The Perfectionist, The Helper, The Achiever, The Individualist, The Investigator, The Loyal Skeptic, The Enthusiast, The Challenger, and the Peacemaker. My favorite books about this topic, *Personality Types* and *The Wisdom of the Enneagram*, both by Don Riso and Russ Hudson, describe how each type has Unhealthy, Average, and Healthy manifestations. In other words, just identifying your type doesn't tell you immediately "how you are." You also need to assess your relative level of health within that type. Most leaders, most organizations, and most families operate at an Average level of health. This means there is a lot of room for growth. To give you a taste of how this works, here are quick-and-dirty summaries of three different Enneagram types that I've lifted from *Personality Types*.

- *Type One: The Reformer.* The key motivation is to be right, have integrity, and be consistent with their ideals. At the highest level of Health they "become extraordinarily wise and discerning...Humane, inspiring, and hopeful. [At an Average level,] dissatisfied with reality, they become high-minded idealists, feeling that it is up to them to improve everything...They point out how things 'ought' to be...Become orderly and well-organized but impersonal, rigid, emotionally constricted...highly critical both of self and others... [At an Unhealthy level they] make very severe judgments of others, while rationalizing their own actions... [They are] condemnatory, punitive and cruel in order to rid themselves of whatever they believe is disturbing them."

- *Type Six: The Loyal Skeptic.* The key motivation is to have safety and security. At the highest level of Health they "become self-affirming, trusting of self and others [which] leads to true courage, positive thinking, leadership, and rich self-expression... [At an Average level they] start investing their time and energy into whatever they believe will be safe and stable...Constantly vigilant, anticipating problems... [They have s]trong self-doubt as well as suspicion about others' motives... [At an Unhealthy level they] become clingingly dependent and self-disparaging with acute inferiority feelings...Feeling persecuted, that others are 'out to get them,' they lash out and act irrationally, bringing about what they fear."

- *Type Nine: The Peacemaker.* The key motivation is to have serenity and peace of mind. At a Healthy level they are "optimistic, reassuring, supportive: have a healing and calming influence—harmonizing groups, bringing people together. A good mediator, synthesizer, and communicator... [At an Average level they] become self-effacing and agreeable, accommodating themselves, idealizing others and 'going along' with things to avoid conflict...Become passive, disengaged, unreflective, and inattentive... [They p]ractice wishful thinking and wait for magical solutions... [At an Unhealthy level they] do not want to deal with problems: become depressed and listless, dissociating self from all conflicts. Neglectful and dangerously irresponsible."[42]

I trust you won't try to identify your type from these brief descriptions. That requires more thorough exploration. Instead, I invite you to notice the wide variation in motivation between just these three types. They are very different! That's the great thing about pinpointing what makes you tick: it suggests very specific practices for becoming a healthier version of your personality type and therefore increasing your odds of practicing great leadership.

Another useful tool for working with your Achilles' Hell is the Hogan Development Inventory (HDI) which identifies "the dark side of personality—qualities that emerge in times of increased strain and can disrupt relationships, damage reputations, and derail peoples' chances of success."[43] The HDI measures personality along 11 scales like Excitable, Skeptical, Leisurely, and Colorful. One thing I like about the HDI is that it consciously builds upon the Center for Creative Leadership's pioneering research on derailment by making the derailers identifiable.[44]

HEALING YOUR ACHILLES' HEEL

What do you do after you've honed in on your Achilles Heel? Both the Enneagram and HDI provide a wealth of answers. Here are my suggestions:

1. As you consider each outer practice of great leadership, ask yourself, *"How might my Achilles' Heel get in the way of successfully taking on this practice?"* For example, as someone who identifies with Type Six (The Loyal Skeptic) on the Enneagram, I find that my pattern of seeing what could go wrong puts me at risk of the following: putting a damper on conversations for possibility by pointing out risks, turning against others when I fear I cannot trust them, getting stuck in complaints, taking my assessments to be the truth, assuming some relationships will never improve, only telling stories that confirm a pessimistic view of the future, getting distracted from listening by worst-case scenario thoughts, and asking mediocre questions because I'm afraid the great ones will blow people away.

2. *Take on new inner practices that elevate you to the healthier levels* of your personality type (in the case of the Enneagram). For me, this includes what Martin Seligman calls *universalizing the positive* and *particularizing the negative.*[45] When something positive happens, like I give a great speech, I have two options: particularize it by telling myself, "I got lucky" or "That was an easy audience" or universalize it by thinking to myself, "I'm a good speaker." Universalizing the positive reinforces my sense of competence and confidence and therefore erodes negative thinking. A similar principle applies when something negative happens. Let's say I trip on a flight of stairs. I can universalize this by calling myself "clumsy," or I can particularize this by thinking, "oops, slipped, no biggie." Particularizing the negative reinforces my resilience and builds a sense of myself as capable.

3. *Observe your Achilles' Heel in action.* What triggers it? How does it operate? If you do this with candor and humility, you may start calling B.S. on yourself, the subject of the next chapter.

CHAPTER 19
CALLING B.S. ON YOURSELF

"I DIDN'T KNOW I had it in me. There's more to all of us than we realize."

—Queen Latifah

Knowledge of your Achilles' Heel has an additional benefit. It allows you to do unto yourself what you like to do unto others: call B.S.

For those new to this term or from other cultures, that means call bullshit. In polite parlance: point out that someone is full of—and deluding—himself.

Calling B.S. on yourself is an unnatural act. Like many of the other practices in this book, it isn't something you've been taught, nor is it something that comes easily to you. This changes once you develop the habit of recognizing your conditioned patterns of thinking and reacting. Suddenly you start to see what was previously invisible to you: how these patterns distract you from being present. You're there in your body, but not really; how else to explain all those days and nights working through exhaustion? You're there with other people, but not fully; after all, what good is an overactive mind if it can't interfere with your awareness of others' experiences?

A few examples of what might prompt you to call B.S. on yourself. You realize that:

- The instinct to be strong and avoid vulnerability blocks you from seeing all the ways you overpower and intimidate people.
- The urge to know everything blocks your curiosity about what others think and what this reveals about them.
- The obsession with success pushes you to race around people without building a single authentic relationship.
- The preoccupation with worst-case scenarios blinds you to the beauty and joy you could be experiencing at this very moment
- The pressure to be correct about everything twists your body into a stiff pretzel that cannot relax much less enjoy all the fun stuff happening around you

Every time you catch yourself in such a pattern, you stop and wonder *What the hell is going on here? And, incidentally, who is running this show?*

Over time, it becomes increasingly difficult to make the case that somebody else is to blame. Like a compact fluorescent light bulb that takes a second to illuminate after the switch has been flipped, your mind eventually has an odd realization: the person running this show is you. It's not the best version of you. It's not you expressing your highest potential. Instead, it's the currently available version, the one calling the shots most of the time.

At this moment, as the light of awareness brightens, a voice deep within you rises from the depths of your being and calls out in a forceful yet loving tone:

Bullshit!

You smile. Who ever thought you'd be calling B.S. on yourself?

As my late grandmother, Thelma, would often say in her New York Jewish accent, "In a million years, who ever heard of such a thing?"

Well, there is a first time for everything.

And here's the surprise: calling B.S. on yourself fills you with energy and a feeling of great possibility. Not because it's pleasant to finally name the weird things you do, but because the person who is naming this weirdness is a deeper and better version of yourself. This is the truth-seeking better angel of your nature. This is the one who can rise to the challenge of great leadership.

CHAPTER 20
MANAGING COMMITMENTS

"YOUR MIND IS for having ideas, not holding them."
—David Allen, *Getting Things Done*

This book doesn't contain a chapter about managing time because I don't know how to manage time. The clock proceeds at the same pace no matter what I'm doing. But I do have something to say about managing commitments, specifically commitments to yourself.

Declaring a new possibility for yourself or your organization is huge. It opens new avenues, particularly when combined with many of the other practices I've described. But what happens to everything you were doing before you declared a new possibility and before you decided to take on new practices? It would be nice to think that all of the old stuff just vanishes—Poof!—but you know better. This stuff hangs around as calendar items, projects, activities, and action items. It's just like those three boxes of cookies you bought before you decided to cut down on the sugar. They're still in the cupboard, and if nothing else changes, you're bound to open them up and munch on a few tasty treats as you are accustomed to doing.

Managing commitments to yourself is the meat and potatoes of great leadership. It's the domain in which you make choices about what to stop doing, what to start doing, and how to makes these shifts without overloading yourself, underloading yourself, or staying up all night.

This topic is key in two overlapping areas:

1. Managing your calendar.
2. Designing and using a trusted system (including but going way beyond your calendar) for managing everything that matters to you.

MANAGING YOUR CALENDAR

One way to manage commitments is through the calendar. This activity invites more excuses, rationalizations, and white lies than just about any other I've encountered. I see this happening often with people trying to take on the practices of great leadership. A few examples:

- A senior executive tells me he'd like to hire me as a coach but is "too busy right now." A year later he hires me. We work really well together. He rises to my challenge and gratefully accepts my support. He actually starts to speak, listen, and think differently. This produces a demonstrably positive impact on his team. However, it's not enough. He doesn't mend all the bridges that have needed mending, so his detractors eventually pull him down. He gets asked to leave the company. "I wish I had started working with you a year earlier," he laments. I can't bring myself to remind him that this is precisely how long he postponed the start of our work. Two questions linger in my mind. First, what exactly was he so busy doing that he ignored the actions most critical to his own career success? Second, why didn't he adjust his calendar to reflect these priorities?

- I'm helping a middle manager prepare for a big presentation. As the date gets closer, it becomes clear to me that she's not giving the project the time and attention it deserves. I finally challenge her to take a hard look at her calendar. "It's time," I say, "to shift the burden of proof onto each event on your calendar: is this essential to do now? If not, cancel it or reschedule." She cancels 75% of her events over the next week. The presentation turns out reasonably well—not as well as if she had done this earlier but much better than if she had kept her calendar intact.

- An executive tells his coach that he has no time on his calendar next week for scheduling important conversations that the coach has assigned as a practice. A half hour later, while working with the executive's assistant to schedule coaching meetings, the coach discovers that the next week's calendar contains many free blocks of time. What is going on here? Amnesia? Deceit? Either way, it's fair to assume that the reason the executive is refusing to schedule those conversations isn't because of time, but because he expects the conversations to be uncomfortable.

Like budgets and bank statements, calendars reveal what's important to you. If something you value is not on your calendar, one of two things is true: either you're managing it from a checklist of some sort or you're simply not doing it. That's the genius of having someone look at your calendar with a curious eye. In the words of Chris Argyris, it shows you not your espoused theory of what you care about, but your "theory-in-use," the one that's actually functioning every day.[46]

Comparing the contents of your calendar to your commitments is not the same thing as changing your calendar to reflect these commitments. However, it is a monumental leap forward. As you become aware of how poorly your calendar reflects your commitments—which is a common phenomenon—a new possibility presents itself. You can take charge of your calendar. As with your complaints and your Achilles' Heel, instead of it owning you, you can begin to own it.

When somebody I coach first catches sight of this possibility, there is one thing I consistently do: get her assistant involved. Although I'm happy to take a quick look at the calendar as part of scheduled coaching meetings, the assistant's job is to manage that calendar every day. The first thing we do is get aligned about the current state of the calendar and how to improve it. (*Wouldn't it be nice if*_____?) Then, I encourage the executive and her assistant to make this priority-setting an ongoing part of their calendar discussions.

I once had an idea for improving the return on investment from executive development. Don't just get a bunch of high potential leaders together. Include their assistants part of the time. Give these pivotal people an opportunity to be with their managers not just in executing on powerful "aha" experiences, but also while actually having those experiences. Let the assistants witness the power of these insights and get a tangible sense of how hard it is to act on them. In reality, many assistants are more aware of these matters than their bosses, so think of this activity as a way to fully enroll them in their bosses' new commitments. That way, they are even more likely to stand firm about tough calendar decisions when their bosses waver. After all, in the kingdom of calendaring, the assistant is queen (or king).

DESIGNING AND USING A TRUSTED SYSTEM

Many commitments don't appear on a calendar. They show up in a variety of systems for tracking activities, projects, promises, and actions. The most common albeit least sophisticated system is a "To Do" list coupled with the manager's memory. Do you remember the first time you created a To Do list? Mine had to do with mowing the lawn. Do you use one now? If so, how would you describe the results it is giving you?

For many years, I took great pride in my To Do list. Having it and using it meant that I was an organized person. Plus it helped me remember to do things. The only problem was that it didn't actually work that well. Before the age of PDAs and smart phones, I had to remember to carry it around with me. Even after technology changed, the more successful I was at keeping the list accurate, the harder it became to find the things I could actually do in that place at that time. Too many items to sort through! In addition, it was hard to track things that other people had promised to me. Where do those go on a To Do list? Finally, putting stars next to things that were important and/or urgent didn't help me decide what to do when the amount of time I had was insufficient for the task. Although I didn't admit it for many years, the To Do list wasn't serving me anywhere near as much as I needed it to.

Then one day my friend Michael Dolan called me up to say he had accepted a job with the David Allen Company.[47] I had heard the name and remembered seeing Allen's book, *Getting Things Done*, on the shelf. But I'd never actually opened it.

I like to understand what my friends are doing, particularly when it's roughly related to my own work. This seemed to fit the bill, particularly when I noticed the book's subtitle, *The Art of Stress-Free Productivity*. There was no doubt in my mind I could become more productive, and I'm always open to ways to reduce stress. So I read the book.

A good decision!

I quickly learned that Getting Things Done (known widely as GTD) has two important virtues: it's powerful, and it's practical. The heart of GTD is creating a trusted system for identifying what matters to you, translating these things into projects and "next physical actions," and taking action on them.[48] I encourage you to look at the book or David Allen's web site. What you will find is a nifty system that:

- *Clears the mind* of concerns, questions, actions, and projects by providing a trusted system for storing this information. Sometimes I like to joke that GTD is better at clearing the mind than meditation. The two together are like Jordan and Pippen: unstoppable. Personally, I use a GTD-friendly application called Evernote that works seamlessly with my Mac and iPhone.

- Invites you to distinguish *actionable* items from non-actionable items. Not everything on your mind actually has to happen! The best way to determine this is to ask, "Is this actionable?"[49]

- Provides specific guidance on how to store non-actionable items that are worth keeping. My physical *reference system* improved dramatically when I started organizing all of my physical files in alphabetical order and labeling them with high quality printed labels. My electronic reference system became much easier to use when I stopped creating 24-layer nests of folders and files and chose instead to label files with the subject heading followed by a hyphen and the topic name. For example: Clients—Ernst & Young/Jane Smith—Contract0908 rather than Clients/Ernst & Young/Jane Smith/Contracts/Sept08. Two layers of hierarchy instead of four means fewer clicks of the mouse, i.e. less time spent on a non-value-added activity.

- Encourages you to translate murky ideas and concerns into *next physical actions*—tangible steps you will take—and "desired outcomes" for multi-step projects. For example, if your mind is preoccupied with thoughts about a report you recently wrote, you'll type or write "XYZ Report Checkup" in the Inbox. Later, you may identify a next action as "Email Tabitha about distribution of XYZ report." Or, alternatively, you'll realize it's a multi-step project and call it "Final draft of report distributed to entire team." Then you can list the next action needed to produce this outcome and others that come to mind.

- Reminds you that you don't have to undertake every physical action yourself. Your other options are to *delegate* it to another person or *defer* it to a later time using your calendar or a tickler system of reminders.

- Forces you to categorize and sort physical actions by *context* like "Home," "Errands," "Phone," and "Office." That way, when you're in the car, you can take a quick look at the Errands list and not get distracted by everything else. When you're at home, you can easily see what needs to be done there.

- Gives you a way of tracking commitments others have made to you (the *Waiting For* list) and stuff that interests you but isn't a current commitment (the *Someday Maybe* list, which also could be called the *Guilt Removal List*.)

- Challenges you to keep your trusted system up to date by holding *Weekly Reviews*, *Dumpster Days* (when you purge your desk, files and cabinets—a very energizing act!), and regular mind dumps in which you clear your thoughts by entering them into your GTD system.

Everyone I know who has tried GTD has enjoyed it, and many swear by it. Lately, I've been considering making it a required part of every coaching program. However, it's not uncommon for managers to start using GTD but not sustain it. Older habits of managing commitments—or avoiding them—return. The To Do list strikes back. Managers love how GTD works but see it as a burden, even though it relieves more burden than it generates. Most importantly, they say they'd love to continue this system, but it takes energy, and they're just too darn tired.

What do you say to someone who cannot manage their system of managing commitments because they're exhausted? "My friend, it's time to manage your physical energy!" This is the topic of the next chapter.

CHAPTER 21
MANAGING PHYSICAL ENERGY

"IF ONE THING is evident about the hectic pace, the orientation to action, the variety and fragmentation of activities of managing, it is the enormous amount of energy that effective managers bring to their work. This is no job for the lazy."

—Henry Mintzberg, *Managing*[50]

Managing may not be a job for the lazy, but it's also not a job for people who are exhausted. Sound like you? If so, it's likely that nowhere in your management education were you taught (a) how much your performance depends upon creating and sustaining physical energy or (b) what enhances your physical energy and what depletes it.

There is a simple reason why you never learned this from mentors, managers, classes, and books: talking about physical energy entails focusing on the body, and nearly every recognized theory of management says not a word about the body. Not a single word.

I find this more than slightly insane.

We can do better. This is why as a coach I start most client meetings by doing a leadership vital signs check. I ask people questions that I'm being paid too much money to ask but that, if unasked, will interfere with the success of coaching: *How's your physical energy level today? How many hours of sleep have you been getting? How many days have you exercised in the past week? What have you been eating lately?*

I'm not embarrassed to ask these questions, but I do like to explain why they matter: "Ching, as you know, the reason we're spending time on this is that if you have no physical energy, everything else we do together will be a waste." I really believe this—and I've seen it come true. One day I'm providing great coaching to a leader, but he's not getting anything out of it because he's wiped out. So I give him a practice related to sleep. Two weeks later, my coaching hasn't improved one iota, nor has the challenge before him shrunk, yet he is suddenly thriving. What's up with that? He's refueled.

Do you remember the last time you felt absolutely energized? Maybe it was this morning. Or maybe it was months ago. Whatever the case, I'd like to help you rebuild your physical energy so that it supports you in practicing great leadership—and, frankly, so that you feel more alive, which has value unto itself. I'll do that by describing four dimensions of physical energy: sleep, exercise, nutrition, and renewal.

SLEEP

"Like a drunk, a person who is sleep-deprived has no idea how functionally impaired he or she truly is."
—Charles Czeisler, Harvard Medical School[51]

According to the National Sleep Foundation, 95 percent of us need 7-8 hours per night. Think you need only 5? Maybe you are superhuman. However, research shows that superhuman performers in many fields get *more* sleep than everyone else. A more likely explanation is that you are deceiving yourself. Has it been so long since you got a good night's sleep that you forgot how it actually feels to be fully rested?

I've never been an outstanding sleeper. In fact, it takes concerted effort for me just to sleep adequately. As a result, I've invested a fair amount of time learning about what keeps me from sleeping well and how to remedy the situation. A couple of years ago, I went so far as to purchase a nighttime sleep monitor called the Zeo. Every night for two months, I went to bed wearing a wireless, sensor-equipped headband that tracked how long it took me to fall asleep, how many times I woke up each night (including tiny awakenings I never noticed), and how much I got of each type of sleep (light, deep, and REM). At the end of the measurement period, it was clear that I was sleeping less and waking up more than I had assumed. So I started hunting for understandings of why I wasn't sleeping any better and what to do about it. Here are a few things I learned:

- Getting to sleep and staying asleep are both important, because *uninterrupted sleep* allows the body to rejuvenate and the mind to learn. Let's say you average eight hours per night but wake up three times with an overactive mind and once to use the restroom. In the morning, your body will not feel rested, and your brain will have missed out on the complex learning that happens during REM sleep.

- There are specific things you can do to *fall asleep* more easily. One is to stick to a consistent bedtime and precede it with a common bedtime ritual. An effective ritual will exclude work, email, TV, alcohol, caffeine, controversy, and anything that gets you revved up. Also important is the physical environment. Is the place you sleep quiet and dark? Do your mattress and pillow meet your needs? Small things like these can make a big difference.

- There are other specific things you can do to *return to sleep* quickly when you wake up. If your mind is filled with thoughts, write them down. Take thirty seconds to stretch your back, shoulders and legs. Learn one of the thousands of simple techniques for relaxing your body. One of my personal favorites is tensing and then relaxing every muscle in my body, starting in the head and moving down the body to the feet.

- *Sleep loss is cumulative.* If you only sleep five hours per night for a week, one night of sleeping ten hours isn't going to cut it. Your cumulative sleep deficit is 21 hours (three hours per night for seven nights), so it will take more than ten ten-hour sleep nights to catch up.

- *Power naps* make a difference. Fifteen years ago, I read that Bill Clinton started to power nap when he learned that his hero, JFK, took power naps—and JFK learned this from his hero, Winston Churchill. That very afternoon, I took my first 20-minute power nap. Actually, it was a 40-minute activity: 20 minutes to fall asleep and 20 minutes of actual nap time. Several months of practice later, I learned to fall asleep in two to three minutes. Now a 20-minute power nap is like grabbing a quick snack between meetings. Fast and effective.

For a full understanding of how you sleep, I recommend *The Promise of Sleep* by the pioneering sleep researcher William Dement. For practical tips on how to fall asleep more easily, surf the web. The Quantified Self movement ("self-knowledge through numbers") is filled with people experimenting with new ways to live a healthy life, including getting quality sleep. As with many of the practices I've introduced, try out a bunch of stuff and watch closely to see what works for you.

EXERCISE

Like many kids my age, growing up meant running around outside and playing a lot of sports. My favorite sport—and my first love in life—

155

was soccer. I started playing in fourth grade when a new kid in town dropped a black-and-white ball on the grass and started kicking it around. *That's a strange looking kickball*, I thought to myself. So I asked him, "What is that?" "A soccer ball," he replied. "Come, and I'll show you how to play." Before I knew it, I had completely lost interest in kickball and was playing pickup soccer games every day after school until dark. The boy who showed me how to play, Seth, was an excellent player, and he introduced me to many other good players. After three hours of soccer every day for a few months, I got pretty good. By the end of the year, when the city held its annual "travel league" tryouts, I received the second highest score among a few hundred kids.

Something else happened, too. I got in really good shape. Keeping up with Seth and the other players hour after hour built muscles and stamina. And once I started playing on a competitive team that practiced regularly, I got in even better shape. It was wonderful, particularly since getting conditioned wasn't the purpose of soccer. It was a by-product. The purpose was to have fun and to win (not always in that order).

What does this make you think of in your own life? Have you ever had the experience of getting in great shape doing something you love rather than purely to get in shape?

If you're like me, it may have been awhile. I have friends and colleagues who continue to play competitive sports into their 40s and 50s, but they are an exception. Most people I know get in shape by *trying* to get in shape. Lifting weights, going out for a run, or getting on the Stairmaster can provide intrinsic fulfillment, but only if you approach these exercises in a very particular way. For most people, working out for the sake of working out often feels more like a chore. Sure, it feels great *after* you are finished, but the activity itself can feel dull and/or painful. Does this sound familiar? Wouldn't it be nice if getting in shape felt engaging or at least less arduous?

I find it helpful to answer each question separately: first, if it were possible to make working out more joyful and engaging, how would you do this? Second, if your goal were, more modestly, simply to stay in shape regardless of how fun the experience is, how might you do that?

Here are ideas for making exercise more engaging:

- *Do something you have always loved doing* but perhaps haven't done much lately. Is it soccer or tennis? Perhaps racquetball or basketball? Swimming? Or maybe going out dancing? (This very evening, my wife and I are going out for high-energy dancing at a club that caters to the over-40 crowd).

- *Try something new that looks fun.* Recently, my friend, Jordan S. Gruber, introduced me to rebounding, which he describes as "bouncing up and down on a high-quality rebounder or mini-trampoline."[52] For eleven years he has bounced while listening to music, lifting hand weights, and even talking to his clients on the phone. Whether or not this is a fit for you, it's helpful to opening your mind to new possibilities.

- *Focus fully on the activity itself.* For many years I would read or watch TV while riding the Elliptical machine or stationary bike. The idea was to "pass the time." One day I realized that the time was certainly passing, but I was missing what was happening. Rather than being "in my body," I was somewhere else. So I switched to what some call mindful workouts. While I'm lifting weights (my primary physical practice these days), my attention is devoted to two things: the movement and my breath. That's it. In between sets or circuits, I like to pause for 60 seconds to take deep breaths and let go of the tension that has built up in my body. Sometimes my body gets so relaxed and present that I actually feel the warmth of the air and hear the sounds of passing cars or the leaves outside rustling in the wind. These are moments of feeling fully alive. Just think of it: pumping iron and meditating at the same time. Who would've thought?

These are a few ideas for making "getting fit" more engaging. I encourage you to try them, discover others, and invent your own. My hunch is you'll find one that creates this new possibility for you.

But what if it doesn't? That brings us to Plan B. Let's assume for the moment that getting fit will never be any more fun or engaging than it is today. How can you ensure that it happens regularly so you get the physical, emotional, and psychological benefits you need to practice great leadership?

Here are several insights that have produced significant shifts in the leaders I coach:

- *A short workout is better than no workout.* OK, so your ideal workout length is 60 minutes. Great. If you only have 20 minutes, are you going to excuse yourself for the day, or are you going to ask, *What can I do in 20 minutes?*

- *Aerobic training* is better than no training, but *anaerobic training* (that draws on lactic acid, not oxygen) is at least as useful. If you run or use an Elliptical machine, switch from a long continuous pace to interval training (short bursts of intense activity followed by rest). You'll burn more fat and do it in less time. Better yet, consider resistance training using weights.

- *Physically getting into workout clothes* dramatically increases the odds you'll actually work out. It's another great Jedi Mind Trick. Give it a try.

- *Don't depend on a single location.* If your gym is 20 minutes away, don't make your gym the only place you work out. Get equipment at home. See what's available at your workplace. Or create a workout that requires no equipment whatsoever.

- *Get a workout buddy.* I prefer training alone, but many others find it helpful to go to the gym or go out for a run with a close friend or possibly someone who is exclusively a workout buddy.

NUTRITION

Our scientific understanding of nutrition has evolved dramatically over the past two decades. If you're still eating what you ate in the mid 1990s, you're probably not giving your body enough sustained energy and may be building up unnecessary body fat. Until a few years ago, I thought that a "low fat" diet was key, until I learned the difference between healthy and unhealthy dietary fats and realized how quickly sugar and other "fast carbs" convert to body fat.

Here are a few other lessons I've learned:

- *Anything that causes your body's energy to spike and then crash* is worthy of your attention. This includes obvious culprits like caffeine and sugar. It also includes more subtle villains like "fast carbs": carbohydrates that quickly break down into simple sugars and elevate blood glucose levels. One example: white potatoes, which are a complex carb *and* fast. What matters most for blood sugar level is not the complexity of the carb but whether it is fast like white potatoes and white rice or slow like broccoli, spinach, and brown rice.

- *Junk food that makes you feel lousy afterwards*—take a look at that, too. What makes this difficult is that it's possible you are so out of touch with your body sensations that you don't notice. For example, I once loved dipping french fries into a Wendy's Frosty. What a combination! I knew it wasn't good for me, but, boy, did it taste good. Then one day I actually paid attention to the experience. Here is what I found. Anticipating the treat was great. The first few bites were amazing. The next few bites, a little less so. By the time I got to the bottom of the Frosty cup, the experience was just OK. Thirty minutes later, little aches and discomforts appeared in my body. Yummy switched to Yucky just like that.

- *Eat to create the emotional experience you want* in two hours rather than to resolve the emotions you feel now. Anyone who has tried to lose weight quickly learns that when they're feeling sad, anxious or angry, food can become a way to "fix" the pain. The purpose is to get out of whatever it is you are currently feeling. A radically different approach is to consider not what you want to escape but what you want to create.[53] How would you like to feel in two hours so you can work and live at your best? What foods will support you in having this feeling? Hint: it's probably not french fries and a Frosty.

- *Remember the difference between dietary fat and body fat.* We need a lot of dietary fat and can eat a lot of it (the "good" kind) without increasing our body fat. In contrast, body fat is something many of us want to reduce. In 2011, I was shocked to learn that my body fat was 24.5 percent. Most of it was "organ" fat and therefore invisible to others. My body produced it because for years my diet was low in fat but high in fast carbs.

- *Remember, too, the distinction between healthy and unhealthy dietary fats.* The good kind includes the monounsaturated fats in olive oil and most nuts and the polyunsaturated fats in fatty fish like salmon and tuna. Omega 3s, a polyunsaturated fatty acid, are particularly good for you.

- Don't buy food marketed as "low fat" or "gluten-free" without *looking at the other ingredients*. Odds are good that the food is filled with processed sugar that can quickly end up as body fat.

- *Eat foods that taste good and are good for you.* Take a look at anything Jonny Bowden has written. I like *The 150 Healthiest Foods on Earth.* This book convinced me to eat a lot of avocados—great taste and a healthy fat. Consider other approaches like the Paleo Diet.

- *Watch how much you eat.* Two reasons: (1) too much of even relatively healthy food can leave you sluggish and (2) research shows you probably eat more than you think. As I searched for ways to eat less, I ran across Dan Buettner's book *Blue Zones.* Buettner takes a close look at why some regions of the world like Okinawa and Sardinia have an unusually large percentage of centenarians (people over 100 years old). One practice shared by many is that they eat less. Some use smaller plates. Others eat until they are no longer hungry, rather than until they're full. The Okinawans set an intention before the meal to practice "Hara hachi bi," or stop eating when their stomachs are 80 percent full.[54] Personally, I come from a family where people always ask, "Have you had enough to eat?" The implication of this question: Eat more! Piggybacking off of the Okinawan practice, I prefer to be asked, "Have you hit the 80 percent mark yet?"

RENEWAL

"Periodization refers to the way athletes train in cycles—alternating intense work with periods of recovery daily, weekly, yearly—in an effort to marshal the highest energy for key competitive events. We believe leaders and their teams need to think in similar terms."[55]

—Tony Schwartz, *Be Excellent at Anything*

In our discussion of managing your calendar, we left out one important piece: creating time for renewal. The research shows that peak performers in sports and the performing arts make conscious and calculated use of renewal periods. They only train or work a certain amount each day. Anything more than that taxes their bodies. They alternate periods of intensity with periods of down-time over the course of a week. They also give themselves extended breaks over the course of a year. Recently, I heard an Olympic alpine skier describe a big difference between herself and her teammate, Picabo Street. This skier trained harder for longer, but Picabo took more breaks. Picabo won the medals.

In his outstanding book, *Be Excellent at Anything*, Tony Schwartz lays out the research case for renewal. He advocates for "setting a new rhythm" in organizations, one that embraces renewal as a business necessity and measures what employees produce rather than how long they work.[56] This aligns well with the idea that organizations give people more flexibility with their time as an expression of trust and as a bottom line imperative. Schwartz takes it a step further by proposing that organizations actively encourage people to periodically pause from intense activity to take breaks. His success helping major companies like Sony put these ideas into practice is a testimony to the value of renewal. I'd go so far as to say that great leadership itself depends upon people getting enough down-time so they have the physical energy to discover new possibilities and bring them to fruition.

Drawing upon Schwartz's recommendations and my clients' experiences, I offer the following tips for renewing yourself:

- *Take a break every 90 minutes.* This is the longest period of intense activity that our bodies can tolerate before we diminish our reserves. At the very minimum, get up out of your chair, go for a walk, and have a glass of water. Even better, take what my colleague Sean Casey LeClaire calls a "body-centered break." His web site[57] includes several 2-minute guided breaks that will clear your mind and relax your body. Alternatively, there are a number of good apps for concentrated breathing exercises and many basic yoga and stretching practices that can shift your energy and emotional state in minutes.

- *Don't multitask.* Multitasking is a misnomer. In reality, when you're doing three things "at once," you're doing a little of one, then a little of the other. Some call this micro-tasking. It may sound impressive, but it drains attention and energy. Rather than simply bash multitasking, I've invented an alternative that I call *uni-tasking for multiple purposes*. Let me give you a personal example. One day I was reading a book to my three-year-old son and thought to myself, *This is taking a lot of time. I could be practicing that speech I'm going to give.* I started to feel frustration. Then I realized my mind had created a false choice between practicing my speech and reading to my son. Wouldn't it be nice if I could do both at the same time? It seemed like a crazy idea until I remembered that half of speech practice involves volume, tone, and body gestures. All of these things are part of reading children's books; they're unavoidable. So I decided to use the experience of reading to my son to practice shifting my volume, tone, and gestures. At first he looked at me and said, "Daddy, what the heck is that? Read normal!" Soon, he accepted this as one of his father's many idiosyncrasies, and reading to him hasn't been the same since. Uni-tasking for multiple purposes! Wouldn't it be great to find ways to do this at work?

What's the one thing you can do to increase your physical energy? Is it turning off the laptop an hour before bedtime? Or is it eating less and better food for dinner?

Whatever it is, start doing that today.

CHAPTER 22
POSTURING

"THE BODY NEVER lies."
—Martha Graham

Posturing, according to the dictionary, means "trying to impress or mislead others." That doesn't sound like a promising route to great leadership. When I speak of posturing, I mean something very different. Here is my personal definition:

Posturing (Verb): Adjusting your body posture to evoke possibility in yourself and others

This new definition is both familiar and strange. The part about adjusting your body to affect others sounds like our old friend, body language. If you cross your arms, people interpret this to mean that you are closed to their ideas. If you scrunch your nose a certain way, they sense you are feeling disgust toward their thoughts and/or toward them (which is often hard to differentiate). In contrast, an open posture and a warm, relaxed facial expression convey to people that you are curious and interested, or at least open and receptive.

This part of Posturing, whether used to positive or negative effect, concerns the impact your body has on others. This is an important topic. For a fun and informative read, I recommend *The Definitive Book on Body Language* by Allan and Barbara Pease. To learn more about the face and what it conveys, the go to person is Paul Ekman. He's the psychologist behind the TV show *Lie to Me* and author of *Emotions Revealed*. Take a look at his web site, which offers online training on how to identify "micro-expressions" and what they mean.

The second half of Posturing is how your body posture affects you *even when nobody is watching*. How you stand, how you hold your head and shoulders, what shape your arms and neck take—these things have an enormous influence on your leadership. They affect your capacity to undertake any of the outer practices of great leadership, like arguing better, turning toward others, or neutralizing enemies.

Here's why: body posture simultaneously reflects and creates a mood (in other words, posture and mood evolve together), and mood influences what's possible in life. Certain postures create positive moods like hope, possibility, and curiosity. Other postures create negative moods like angst, resentment, anger, and resignation. Change your posture, and you can change your mood, or at least increase your odds of doing so.

Try this on for size: cross your arms tightly and hunch your back (unless you have a physical condition that prevents this). Then look up and say, "I'm really excited to be here." Feels awkward, doesn't it? That's because you've put your body in a negative mood while saying something positive. These two parts of yourself are out of alignment. In the real world, this won't happen. What will happen instead in this posture is you'll say something critical and perhaps even destructive, because these words better match the mood your body has evoked.

Now do the opposite: Open your posture by sitting or standing upright, pulling your shoulders back and down, and taking a few deep breaths. Relax your facial muscles and eyes. Say the same thing as before: "I'm really excited to be here." Does that feel easier and more natural? It likely will because your posture now supports the positive mood needed to match your words. You're back in alignment with yourself.

This small experiment suggests that posturing is one of the most fundamental inner practices of great leadership. In a hardheaded moment, I'd say this even more strongly: don't waste your time trying to improve your leadership without simultaneously focusing on your body posture.

Here are three simple steps you can take to get a reading on your current posture:

1. Track your body posture during the day by *observing yourself in action.*

2. *Ask a trusted colleague to watch you* in action and give you immediate feedback, the more specific the better.

3. *Ask your assistant to take unannounced photos* of you during the day at your desk. Before you go home, take a look at the photos. What do you see?

Once you have a clear sense of your current postural habits, spend some time exploring what it feels like to mix things up a bit. What if you were to relax your shoulders downward? What is it like to breathe from your belly rather than your chest? Instead of leaning forward, how about being upright? What happens when you have both feet on the floor?

I can't give you specific suggestions about this because I cannot see you. Even if you were standing right in front of me, I would still make the same suggestion: try out a bunch of stuff and see what works. There is only one way to learn whether relaxing your shoulders downward relaxes you into a state where you can listen like a master: by trying it repeatedly and tracking the results. There is only one way to know whether putting both feet on the floor gives you the feeling of grounded support you need to flip complaints into commitments: by trying it. In the end, the practice of posturing is a great arena for self-experimentation.

We've now explored seven inner practices of great leadership. Which one will have the most value for you? After you have selected an inner practice to go along with the outer practice you consider most valuable, it is time to consider *how* to most effectively take on these practices so that they produce real, sustainable results. This is the subject of Part Four.

HOW TO PRACTICE

Chapter 23
Deliberate Practice

"THE REALITY THAT deliberate practice is hard can even be seen as good news. It means that most people won't do it. So your willingness to do it will distinguish you all the more."
—Geoff Colvin, *Talent Is Overrated*

As we've seen, top performers in sports, music, and the theatrical arts aren't born at elite levels. They achieve remarkable things and develop to their full potential by the actions they take day after day with the intent to improve. The source of their excellence is deliberate practice, which has several key ingredients:

- It is designed specifically to improve performance.
- It can be repeated at high volume.
- The person receives continuous feedback from a teacher or coach.

- It requires intense focus and concentration.
- It may not always be fun.

Because deliberate practice is hard work, not everybody is up for the challenge. You have to be ignited to practice. This ignition often happens in a single powerful moment when you realize on a primal level that you want to be great and will dedicate yourself to getting there. As we saw earlier in the book:

Great Leadership = Ignition + Deliberate Practice

In *Talent Is Overrated*, Geoff Colvin distinguishes between two forms of deliberate practice: *direct practice* and *on-the-job practice*. This distinction is important, because each form of practice suggests a unique approach to developing leadership. Organizations that draw on both direct practice and on-the-job practice are more likely to bring about the results they desire. In other words, our equation now becomes:

Great Leadership = Ignition + Direct Practice + On-the-Job-Practice

DIRECT PRACTICE

The direct or pure form of practice, according to Colvin, can happen using any of the following four approaches: the music approach, in which you break a skill into its parts and practice the parts; the chess approach, in which you replicate situations faced by masters and compare your choices to theirs; the sports conditioning approach, in which you build underlying muscles needed to master a skill; and the sports simulation approach, in which you create simulations of changing circumstances that require fast responses.

Let's say it's time to learn how to argue better. How might you practice this?

- *Music approach.* First break the skill of arguing into its parts. For example: grounding assessments, asking others to ground their assessments, listening with the intent to understand, asking clarifying questions, framing your assessments with powerful declarations, and inquiring what others think of your assessments. Then pick one or two of these components and practice them over and over—not five times, but fifty or a hundred times. To get better, you have to go for volume. And remember to get feedback from a colleague or coach.

- *Chess approach.* This is harder because leadership masters generally don't leave clear trails of their conversations, and certainly not of their arguments. (In contrast, if the skill is public speaking, that's something you *can* replicate and compare). So improvise. Find someone in your organization who is a master at rigorous debate and watch him in action. Take detailed notes of who said what. Then, in a quiet space on your own or with a partner, repeat their words and gestures. The idea isn't to *become* him (you can only be you) but to experience what speaking like him *evokes* in you. Maybe, with enough repetition, some of the words and gestures will actually start to feel like you.

- *Sports conditioning approach.* This is the most unorthodox model of practice for leaders. What does it mean to get conditioned to argue well? What are the underlying muscles you need in an argument? In my experience, the muscles in leadership that need to be conditioned are particular human qualities. Listening to understand requires curiosity. Making powerful declarations requires courage. Grounding your assessments calls for rigor. How curious, courageous, and rigorous are you today? Whatever your current levels of competence, there are ways to lift them up a notch. For example, if you're open to yoga, the warrior pose is a great way to build courage into your body. The martial art of aikido shows you how to blend with the energy of an attacker in a

173

way that protects you without hurting them. Likewise, there are specific breathing and relaxation practices to build curiosity and mental focusing exercises to build rigor. Finally, all leaders need physical energy, so my suggestions around nutrition, exercise, sleep, and renewal fit the conditioning approach.

- *Sports simulation approach.* Recruit a few family members to simulate a debate. Give them a part to play and lines to say. The debate could be one from work or a live argument you need to have with them anyhow (like where to go for vacation).

Using these four approaches to direct practice will give you a leg up on nearly everyone else trying to improve their leadership. Employing them in partnership with colleagues will raise the standard for leadership in your organization.

For most leaders, the level of specificity I have provided here is more than sufficient. However, what about leaders who in earlier careers have performed at high levels in sports, music, or the performing arts—and are familiar with a larger bag of tricks for effective practice? How can they use these tricks for leading better? Or let's say you didn't play professional basketball or perform at Carnegie Hall yet are so dedicated to practice that you want to adapt the very best tricks of the trade. What else is possible?

As it turns out, the answer is: a lot. In *The Little Book of Talent*, the follow up and companion manual to *The Talent Code*, Daniel Coyle describes 52 specific tips for developing skills to your full potential. He divides these into three categories: igniting your practice by linking your identity with top performers in your field (getting started), deepening your practice by stretching yourself and using high repetition (improving skills), and sustaining progress when you get stuck.[58] Let's look at a few examples from each category and how you might apply them to the practice of arguing better.

1. GETTING STARTED

- *Spend fifteen minutes a day engraving the skill on your brain*: "Watch the skill being performed, closely and with great intensity, over and over, until [you] build a high-definition mental blueprint."[59] This resembles Colvin's chess approach but with more emphasis on intensity. When you're watching someone argue effectively, focus one hundred percent of your attention on them.

- *Choose spartan physical surroundings over luxurious ones* because "luxury whispers *Relax, you've made it.*"[60] This is the opposite of what organizations generally do, particularly with senior executives. Consider modest settings for practicing how you argue and steer clear of plush resorts.

- *Figure out if you're practicing a hard skill or a soft skill*: "Hard, high precision skills are actions that are performed as correctly and consistently as possible," like swinging a tennis racket, shooting a free throw, or playing a specific chord on a guitar. "Soft, high flexibility skills are those that have many paths to a good result...and are about being agile [like] a soccer player sensing a weakness in the defense and deciding to attack [or] a singer subtly interpreting the music to highlight emotion."[61] Arguing better requires a mix of hard and soft skills. There is the hard skill of speaking with precision and maintaining a consistently relaxed body posture and vocal tone even when you get emotionally triggered. There is also the soft skill of adapting what you say and do to others' words and body language.

2. IMPROVING SKILLS

- *Find the sweet spot:* "There is a place, right on the edge of your ability, where you learn best and fastest [and] where you're fully engaged in an intense struggle—as if you're stretching with all

175

your might for a nearly unreachable goal."[62] Vary when you practice arguing: first thing in the morning or (if you have a willing partner) in the middle of the night. Role play with someone you trust whose presence also leaves you a bit on edge. Pick topics that are complex or contentious. Practice with the lights out or outside in the rain. Be creative.

- *Take off your watch*: "Instead of counting minutes or hours, count reaches and reps."[63] Practice the same subset of a difficult conversation seven times. Have your practice partner say something that bothers you and practice responding calmly and skillfully—and then repeat this, with slight variations, six more times.

- *Slow it down (even slower than you think)*: "Super-slow practice works like a magnifying glass: It lets us sense our errors more clearly, and thus fix them."[64] When practicing by yourself, speak slowly and pause after each sentence. Go back and do it slightly differently. When practicing with a partner, don't try to have the whole argument at once. Do it in small chunks, and pause after each chunk to reflect, assess, and self-correct. Give each other feedback before trying it again or moving on.

3. SUSTAINING YOUR PRACTICE

- *Embrace repetition:* "Instead of viewing it as a chore, view it as your most powerful tool."[65] Commit to regularly practicing how to argue better by visualizing the remarkable results it can produce. Think of it as your secret sauce for great leadership.

- *Don't waste time trying to break bad habits—instead, build new ones:* "Put your energy toward building a new habit that will override the old one."[66] If you tend to shout when arguing, practice speaking at a moderate volume and even tone. If you drone on forever, focus on crispness. If you make ungrounded assessments, practice providing valid evidence. If you tend to cross your arms, find a more comfortable way to hold them—and practice breathing deeply.

- *Cultivate your grit:* "Grit is that mix of passion, perseverance, and self-discipline that keeps us moving forward in spite of obstacles. It's not flashy, and that's precisely the point."[67] View every argument in the workplace or in practice as an opportunity to rise to big challenges. When you mess up by losing your temper or nervously stumbling over your words, don't despair. As quickly as you can, calm yourself and reflect on what happened and what you can do differently next time. And when you excel in an argument, don't just rejoice. Study what happened so you can replicate your success in the future.

ON-THE-JOB PRACTICE

Practicing on-the-job requires not new time but new attention. Your calendar may change a little or a lot. What shifts dramatically is how you show up in these experiences, what you do to prepare for them, and how you learn from them afterwards—through reflecting and getting feedback. Think of these four steps—prepare, act, reflect, and get feedback—as the *on-the-job practice cycle:*

- *Prepare:* what you do before a meeting, speech, email, factory tour, customer visit, negotiation, etc.

- *Act:* the meeting, speech, email, tour, visit, or negotiation itself.

- *Reflect:* what you do afterwards to consider what happened, why and how it happened, and what you can learn from it.

- *Get Feedback:* what you do afterwards to elicit other people's perspectives on what they observed.

If you don't enjoy action, you probably shouldn't be a manager. But if you act 100 percent of the time and never prepare, reflect, or get feedback, you won't be a great manager. Competent, but not great.

This is why it is vital to fully understand the four steps of the on-the-job-practice cycle, the topic of the next chapter.

CHAPTER 24
ON-THE-JOB PRACTICE CYCLE

"PRACTICE ON THE days that you eat."
—Shinichi Suzuki, music education pioneer

PREPARING

In organizations people prepare before they act, but they don't do it particularly well. The preparation is inconsistent, haphazard, not always focused on the events that matter most, and not often done using skillful means.

The most common form of preparation (other than getting dressed in the morning and drinking coffee) is creating meeting agendas. The value of an agenda is most apparent in its absence: conversations are unfocused. They wander. In fact, they can't even go "off track" because there is no track. In contrast, a clear agenda provides discipline and focus.

But there's a problem with agendas: you probably don't use them consistently. For example, take the simple but important example of development conversations. When you meet with direct reports for a development conversation, do you have an agenda? Who creates it? In many organizations, this responsibility falls to the direct report. After all, "they own their careers." But is this a sole ownership—or do you, as their direct manager, hold some responsibility? Even if this isn't in your formal job description, don't you have an opinion about your direct reports' careers and what's possible for them? If so, wouldn't it make sense to allocate some of the development conversation toward this end?

Now, let's assume you start using meeting agendas with greater focus and consistency. Does this make you fully prepared?

Not if you listen to the stories of leaders who are pros at preparation. For them, the creation of an agenda is necessary but not sufficient for meetings and completely irrelevant for activities that involve more improvisational activity. Complete preparation involves getting your head, heart, and gut ready for whatever is going to happen next. I divide this into three categories: *macro-preparing*, which means considering your overall intention and mood going in; *micro-preparing*, which means defining what success looks like and charting how you plan to get there; and *preparing your body*.

MACRO-PREPARING

Assume you have a solid practice of managing commitments and therefore are attending the events you most need to attend. Before you set foot in any particular event, take five minutes to ask yourself the following questions:

1. What would you like this event to accomplish? This is not what you want to achieve, but what you want the group to achieve.

2. What can you contribute to achieving this result? What perspective, what questions, what listening, what ideas? Or maybe the value you can add is to invite a new voice to the conversation.

3. What's your general mood around this event? Are you enthusiastic? Resigned? Resentful? Be honest with yourself. It's a rare manager who doesn't feel resigned or resentful about at least one event on their calendar every day.

4. What assessment is behind this mood? Let's say you feel resigned. Do you think of this group as a waste? Or is it a high-powered group that you assess to be poorly led or heading in a dangerous direction? Perhaps you place a low assessment on your own ability to add value to the group?

5. What can you do to shift yourself into a mood of possibility? Do this.

6. Once you feel more positive, repeat questions 1 and 2 with an emphasis on wondering what is possible.

Ironically, macro-preparing for experiences is more than just an act of preparation. It gives you an opportunity to declare that you care about something and are committed to bringing your best to it. This simple declarative act can do wonders for bringing your full presence to the events on your calendar.

MICRO-PREPARING

If macro-preparing involves declaring what matters to you and why, micro-preparing involves assessing what success looks like and what strategies you will use to get there. Consider asking yourself these questions:

1. Given your intended contribution, how will you know you've been successful? Is there anyone you can ask for feedback to help you make this assessment?

2. Can you visualize what success looks like? Consider doing a visualization exercise to picture things going well.

3. What approach will you take to make this contribution?

4. What could get in the way? How will you handle these challenges?

5. What can you do at the beginning of the event to ensure you are present, centered, and grounded?

6. How will you practice [insert the leadership skill you most need to develop] in this conversation?

7. Is this meeting important enough that you'd like to rehearse in advance? If so, when and with whom?

PREPARING YOUR BODY

The more important the conversation—the higher the stakes and the greater the odds of emotions escalating—the more crucial it is to prepare your body. I find it sad to hear about people who have performed poorly in presentations or meetings because they skipped lunch or forgot to go to the bathroom. To invest so much time, energy, brainpower and heart in an activity and then flub it because you forgot to do something you learned at age five—this is the ultimate preventable bummer.

Preparing your body therefore includes but goes beyond the practices introduced in the chapter on physical energy. Yes, it is useful to get good sleep, get in shape, eat nutritiously, and regularly renew yourself *in general*.

It is also helpful for *particular events* on your calendar to ensure that your body is present, centered, and grounded:

- As you walk into each new room or situation, *take a few long deep breaths.* Feel your feet on the ground. If you're sitting, feel your bottom and back on the seat. Are your legs parallel to the ground? If not, adjust the height of the seat. (A seat at the wrong height affects your posture, and we know what impact that has).

- *Remind yourself of the possibility* you are committed to. A simple phrase or visual image does the trick. One manager I worked with tells himself *relax* before important meetings, and it works: he relaxes and becomes more open and positive.

- *Notice any tension in your body.* Feel a knot in your shoulders? Imagine your breath going straight to the shoulders. Feel the knot's tightness—and then marvel as it gradually softens.

ACTING

After preparation comes action. The one thing I want to say here: make sure to show up, if for no other reason than to give yourself material for reflection and feedback.

REFLECTING

After acting comes reflecting. The great thing about this part of the on-the-job-practice cycle is that it requires only one person—you—and just a bit of time—5-10 minutes—yet can produce extraordinary learning.

In 1973 Henry Mintzberg did something truly revolutionary for a scholar. Instead of just theorizing about the life of managers, he actually followed a bunch of senior executives as they went about their day and took detailed notes of what he saw. Perhaps his most famous observation from that study was that executives at every level work at an unrelenting pace and are continuously interrupted. As one executive told him, managing is "one damn thing after another."[68]

A downside is that most managers spend a very small amount of time reflecting on what they've done and what it means. The job is never done, the pace is unrelenting, and the interruptions are frequent. When is there time to reflect? That's unfortunate, because reflecting is how we see patterns, make sense of our experience, and learn.

Notice I said that "most" managers reflect little. More accurate would be to say "all but the best" managers. In his study, Mintzberg found that "a remarkable number of effective managers are reflective: they know how to learn from their own experience; they explore numerous options; and they back off when one doesn't work, to try another."[69]

Implicit in this notion of reflection is paying attention without judgment. After all, on any given day managers experience unpleasant surprises, encounter uncomfortable situations, and get emotionally triggered. The purpose of reflection is not to wallow in these experiences—or even to triumph in successes—but instead to notice what happened and make sense of it. This can include:

- Making grounded assessments about why something happened.
- Getting a clearer understanding of people you work with and what makes them tick.
- Mapping your own emotional geography, including the early indicators that you are about to get angry or fearful.
- Gaining new insights about how your team functions or how it fits into the larger organization.
- Recognizing political dynamics and the myriad expressions of power and influence.
- Learning about your company's customers and suppliers.
- Reconsidering something that's been nagging you all day in a way that allows you to be at peace with it and/or take effective action.

- Considering what you will do differently tomorrow, next week, and next month.

The genius of reflection is that it is incredibly simple. All you need is a little time, a little quiet, and a few powerful questions. In fact, the questions don't even need to be that powerful. If you find the time and the space, asking one or two half-decent reflective questions produces far better results than skipping the act of reflection entirely.

The questions you can ask yourself include:

- What were you trying to accomplish? In retrospect, was this the best objective, or was there an alternative?
- What strategy or approach did you plan to use to accomplish this? Would another approach have worked better?
- What assumptions about yourself, others, or the situation were behind what you were trying to accomplish?
- What actually happened? What did you do? How did others respond?
- What were the results? How do these compare to your intended results?
- What went well? What part did you play in this?
- What didn't go well? What would you attribute that to?
- What surprised you?
- What was the biggest challenge? How did you handle it?
- How did you practice [insert a skill you are trying to develop]?
- What new possibilities do you now see?
- What emotions are you experiencing as you reflect upon this experience?
- What would you do differently next time?
- What did you learn from this experience?

THREE LEVELS OF LEARNING

As you consider this list of questions, I want you to notice that some invite a deeper level of reflection than others. It's one thing to ask what happened and quite another to ask why it happened and still another to consider the deeper (rather than superficial) causes. A useful way of understanding this distinction comes from Bill Torbert, author of *Action Inquiry: The Secret of Timely and Transforming Leadership*. Torbert describes three forms of learning, which he calls "single loop," "double loop," and "triple loop":[70]

- *Single loop learning*: you respond by changing your behaviors. One question that prompts such learning is "What would you do differently next time?"

- *Double loop learning*: you respond by changing the strategies that lay behind these behaviors. A question you can ask here is "Would another approach have worked better?"

- *Triple loop learning*: you respond by changing the deeper purpose or intention that underlies those strategies. You ask, "What were you trying to accomplish" or, on a deeper level, "What assumptions were behind what you were trying to accomplish?"

This is similar to the Five Whys practice pioneered by Toyota to explore the cause-and-effect patterns behind problems or errors.[71] In both cases, you don't accept superficial explanations for what has happened. You look deeper. The main difference is that whereas the Five Whys typically sticks to behavioral causes, this learning model challenges you to also consider cognitive and emotional causes.

ASSESSING PROGRESS IN REFLECTING

Let's say you begin to incorporate reflection into your day-to-day life. If you're the kind of person who likes to have indicators of progress, you may find yourself asking a question that my clients often put to me: "How do I know I'm getting better at reflecting?"

Now, if you're actually asking yourself this question, you *must* be making progress because you care enough to want to know. To this I say: kudos!

More practically, I like to distinguish three broad stages through which you progress as you build competence at reflection:

1. *No reflection.* You simply move from one action to the next without awareness of what happened or what you can do differently. At the very best, when things go wrong, you see how others, not you, can change.

2. *Reflection after action.* You can look back after the fact, observe your behaviors, and consider what you can do differently.

3. *Reflection in the midst of action.* You can simultaneously behave and observe yourself behaving. Your awareness is in two places at the same time—not easy to accomplish! This is sometimes known as self-observation.

For many years, I asked leaders to reflect in the midst of action. This was never easy for folks. Often, despite their best efforts, it simply didn't happen. The reasons for this remained a mystery to me until I came across research on the stages of development that adults progress through long after their bodies have stopped growing. It turns out that the mind you have at age 55 may not be the same mind you have at age 35. It can be qualitatively different, namely by having a greater capacity to handle complexity and reflect back upon itself. This is not guaranteed to happen, but it *can* happen.

In fact, it doesn't happen for all managers, or all adults, and herein lies the reason many managers have difficulty reflecting. Studies show that approximately 55 percent of managers fall into what I'm calling the *no reflection* category. If and when they look back on what happened, they are unable to see how their own behaviors played a role in negative results. Forty percent of managers are able to do *reflection after action*. Most of this group can see what they might do differently (*single loop learning*) but not why (*double* or *triple loop learning*). Less than 5 percent of managers are able to *reflect in the midst of action*, and of those who can, only a fraction do it consistently.[72]

The upshot of this research is important yet relatively simple: teach people to walk before they run, and don't expect miracles when repeated incremental progress is what matters. So although I still give people "self-observation exercises," my request to them is to pause after action (like at lunch or at the end of the day) to reflect. The measure of success then becomes how consistently they actually follow through and do this reflection. Once or twice a day is a reasonable standard.

Once you build a practice of reflecting, you start to notice all the habits that have been with you for years but were below your level of awareness. The way you habitually act in whatever area you are focusing on (e.g. arguing, telling stories, listening, asking questions) becomes an object in your awareness. As this happens, not only do you start calling B.S. on yourself, but you also start to wonder, "How do I know I'm making progress in becoming more aware of these habits?"

The 360 degree interviews that are part of most coaching engagements provide a reasonably good way to measure this, but they typically happen only once or twice a year. And not everyone has a coach. So I offer the following three metrics that, while not technically measurable, provide a distinction that you may find conceptually useful:

- When you engage in an old habit (e.g. interrupting others, losing your temper, speaking in a confusing way), what percentage of the time do you catch yourself doing this? Ten percent of the time? Half the time? It takes a long time to even get near 100 percent, but higher is always better.

- How long after the old habit occurs do you catch yourself? A minute? An hour? Two weeks? Progress means gradually shortening this amount of time.

- Of the occasions you catch yourself in an old habit, what percentage of the time do you self-correct by instituting new behaviors? Again, it takes a long time to even get close to 100 percent, but higher is better.

Now, let's say you become a superstar at reflecting on your own behaviors and the motivations behind them. This is an extraordinary feat worth celebrating. I would say "take yourself out to dinner," except that it's likely your colleagues will be so happy by the quality of your leadership that they'll take you out to dinner. When this happens, amidst the celebration and adulation, you may find yourself wondering, *How do I know my own reflective observations are accurate? What if others see something very different from me?* Your celebratory dinner isn't the time to ask these questions, but it does point toward the fourth and final step in the on-the-job practice cycle: getting feedback.

GETTING FEEDBACK

Leadership researchers tell us that one of the biggest differentiators between companies that have great leadership pipelines and those that don't is that the former give leaders large and rich amounts of feedback.[73]

The reason for this is rather simple: we need each other. We need each other to be able to see reality not just from one angle, but from many angles. We need each other to illuminate our blind spots so that what was previously hidden becomes visible.

High quality feedback does this. It provides what even the best reflection cannot: a multi-faceted perspective on a highly complex reality. Doing this helps rising stars avoid derailment. It prevents their Achilles' Heels from becoming Achilles' Hell. This is why companies with the best leadership pipelines provide large amounts of quality feedback.

Yet such companies are the exception. Most organizational cultures are either feedback-poor or feedback-predatory. Either you hear nothing of value or you get attacked. Silence or violence. Why is this the case?

Asking for, giving, and receiving feedback are as emotionally difficult as they are logistically simple. When you watch "feedback pros" do this, it looks easy and effortless. In many cases, it is, but only because they've done it a thousand times. You've done it twice. Not a fair comparison!

When you try *asking* for feedback yourself, a broad array of emotional barriers get in the way. Fear of rejection. Regret about what you've done. Embarrassment at placing yourself in the "inferior" role of asking for feedback. And a myriad of other emotions, each matched with an uncomfortable physical sensation.

When you think of *giving* feedback, even when asked, you face the realization that you risk violating the tacit agreements you've made with your colleagues: *If you say nice things to me, then I'll say nice things to you.* There is a reason you've made such agreements: you fear that if you are honest with your colleague, they will be more candid with you. And you're not sure you want that! Tacit agreements preserve the veneer of collegiality yet sacrifice the learning you get from each other's perspectives.

In paranoid cultures, the situation is even stickier. Shaming and blaming are so endemic that there is reasonable cause for you to feel afraid of asking for feedback and reluctant to give it. If you ask for it, you're likely to get hammered. If you give it, odds are good the other person will respond defensively and even retaliate by sending a bit of "feedback" (not the good kind) back your way.

Ironically, giving and receiving quality feedback is precisely the "medicine" that your organization needs to improve its health. Here's why: good feedback shows you with great precision exactly when you are practicing great leadership—and when you are not. No matter which practices you have taken on, quality feedback provides the best indicator of your progress or lack thereof.

WHAT CONSTITUTES HIGH QUALITY FEEDBACK?

Assuming you're ready to receive more feedback, how do you ensure that it produces the results you desire, namely more learning coupled with stronger relationships? What, indeed, constitutes high quality feedback? In my experience, high quality means specific, requested, ongoing, and real time feedback from a rich variety of competent observers. Let's break this definition down into its component parts so that you can guide others to give you such feedback:

- *Specific.* This means describing visibly observable behaviors. "You raised your voice and clenched your fist" is specific. "You got angry" is not. Such visible behaviors can include your words, body language, facial expression, tone of voice, etc. We can also distinguish specific feedback by its relevance to the particular skill you are practicing. If you are deliberately practicing how to ask great questions, getting feedback about this would be more useful than, say, feedback about the quality of the stories you tell.

- *Requested.* Your colleagues likely feel more comfortable giving their perspectives when you have asked for it and when they are confident that you will listen to them, take their words seriously, and not argue. You request it by saying, "I'd like to get your feedback about how well I asked questions in this afternoon's meeting. All I will do when you give feedback is listen, take notes, and ask clarifying questions." To make this promise credible, you

191

have to follow through. No counter-arguments disguised as questions. Breathing deeply, feeling your feet on the ground, and posturing always help.

- *Ongoing.* Far too many organizations rely on annual performance reviews to tell people how they're doing. Once a year isn't enough, particularly for powerful senior executives who can get caught in bubbles because the only people who feel safe giving them feedback, their bosses, are either too busy or not competent at doing so. Here is a better standard: get feedback at least three times a week from three different sources.

- *Real time.* When I shadow senior managers (follow them around and observe them in action), I like to give them feedback immediately after observing them. The experience is fresh in their memory, and it's fresh in mine. I do this by contracting with them to have a conversation during the small "breaks" in the day. How can you do this if you don't have a coach shadowing you? Ask a trusted colleague to observe a particular behavior during a particular meeting and then give you 60 seconds of feedback in the hallway afterwards or through a short email that same day.

- *Rich variety.* The leadership research suggests that feedback works best when it comes from multiple people who see you in a range of contexts. An executive working on how well she listens might ask a direct report at the end of a 30 minute one on one meeting, "How well do you think I listened to you in this meeting? What could I do better?" Notice how different this is from asking a peer to provide feedback on her listening behaviors in a wide ranging strategic discussion involving twenty people. Both can be revealing, and the combination of the two can produce robust insights.

- *Competent observers.* I've conducted hundreds of 360 degree interviews over the years, and I've noticed that some people are much more skillful at observing people than others. I like to ask, "Can you give me a specific example of what so-and-so did or said? Can you tell me what you observed on their face or in their body language?" Some people provide nuanced details. Others have difficulty providing anything beyond vague adjectives. Many are in between. This makes it challenging to find competent observers, but some are better than none.

The standard for feedback is so low that I like to nudge leaders to stretch beyond what's comfortable. When they demur, I like to say, "If you think this is scary, let me tell about the time I called up six ex-girlfriends and asked them what they thought about me as a boyfriend and what they wished I had done differently." Yes, I have walked this path myself and can attest that a curious mind that musters the courage to ask unusual questions can experience profound learning.

THE NEXT-TO-LAST EQUATION FOR GREAT LEADERSHIP

At the beginning of the book, we learned a simple equation for achieving great leadership:

Great Leadership = Ignition + Deliberate Practice

Then, at the outset of Part Four, we explored the two forms of deliberate practice. This provided more detail to the equation:

Great Leadership = Ignition + Direct Practice + On-the-Job-Practice

Now that we've looked more closely at what it means to practice on the job, we have come to the following:

Great Leadership = Ignition + Direct Practice + Preparation + Action + Reflection + Feedback

In the next chapter, we'll explore one final source of leverage in developing your leadership: the specific challenges you face at work. As we have seen, not all on-the-job experiences are created equal. Some produce more learning and growth than others. This has an important implication for you. As you actively engage in the on-the-job-practice cycle and thereby get better at your job, a new question may enter your mind: is *this* job the best place for me to doing all of this practicing?

CHAPTER 25
SEEKING OUT CHALLENGE

"THE BEST MOMENTS occur when a person's body or mind is stretched to its limits in a voluntary effort to accomplish something difficult and worthwhile."

—Mihaly Csikszentmihalyi

I'm a fan of changing from where you are today rather than lunging after a new job, relationship, or city in a belief it will make you more content or effective. That's why I haven't said anything yet in this book about whether your current job is "the right job" for you at this point in time and, if not, what else might be. I've been more interested in helping you develop yourself *within* your current situation. As we've seen, deciding what parts of great leadership to practice and learning how to practice them can improve the quality of your leadership by freeing you to bring your best.

Now it's time to talk at a higher level of altitude about the actual nature of your work. Here are two reasons why:

1. No matter how you approach your current role as it is now defined (and no matter how well you practice new skills), it may not give you the challenges you need to be fully engaged and rising to your best. Either you've mastered the challenges of the role, or it was never a great stretch for you from the outset.

2. The leadership development research tells us that some experiences are better at producing leadership competence than others. Not all jobs are created equal, and not all ways of scoping a job are equally effective at building the particular kinds of competence your organization needs its future leaders to possess. In other words, even if you're not lacking in challenge, are you encountering the "right" challenges, the ones that will teach you the skills you need to learn?

This brings me to back to the research done by the Center for Creative Leadership (CCL) over thirty years ago and updated in the past decade. As you'll recall, the researchers learned that there is a distinct set of experiences that teach leadership lessons better than others. The original study of white male executives listed 17 experiences. The updated study that included African American and women leaders added six for a total of 23 experiences. Here, again, are five that stand out to me:

- Starting from scratch
- Turnarounds
- Increased scope
- Line-to-staff switch
- Special bosses (very good or very bad)

These five experiences and the rest on the CCL list produce more and better learning for leaders. What does this mean for you?

To begin, it means that we can update our equation for great leadership. In the last chapter, we realized that there are more leverage points in developing ourselves than most people believe. Our equation looked like this:

Great Leadership = Ignition + Direct Practice + Preparation + Action + Reflection + Feedback

Now, it's time to incorporate this final leverage point: the degree of challenge present in your work. To be provocative, I'm going to suggest that introducing the right kinds of challenges—those on CCL's list—has a multiplicative, not additive, effect on leadership. Our final equation (for now, at least!) is this:

Great Leadership = Ignition + (Direct Practice + Preparation + Action + Reflection + Feedback) x Challenge

This means that you can significantly improve your leadership by paying close attention to the types of challenges you face on the job. In case big equations aren't your cup of tea, let's make this really practical. Here is a series of questions for you to ask, hopefully in conversation with your manager and possibly in collaboration with a strategic HR leader:

1. What is the uppermost role you could potentially be hired for?

2. To succeed in this role, what lessons (about the business, about managing, etc?) will you need to have learned from prior experiences?

3. Which of these lessons can you learn from your existing role as currently defined?

4. Which can you not?

5. What combination of new experiences now and in coming years will teach you the additional lessons you need to learn?

6. How can you build these challenging experiences into your existing role? By redefining the role? By taking on a special assignment, joining a task force, or participating on an action learning team?

7. When will it be time to move to a different position?

8. What support structures—like feedback, in-the-moment coaching from your manager, reflective time, support from an external coach, or training that matches your skill focus—can you receive to maximize what you learn from these experiences?

Unless you work for one of the organizations that are true "talent machines," I'll bet good money that nobody has asked you these questions before. Maybe the one about uppermost role, but not the others. So I applaud you for simply being willing to bring these into your field of awareness.

Now, I want to point out two pieces of good news about seeking out challenges. First, building your leadership development strategy around on-the-job experience (among other things) already makes a lot of sense to you—and to your manager and your manager's manager. It's how you assume you have always learned best, right? And so it's likely to be something you're willing to sign up for in the future. The "club" of on-the-job-learning requires no new membership, just the renewal of your existing membership. Second, you probably prefer it to the sophisticated-sounding yet vague language of competencies or the option of heading off to a course that may or may not relate to what you're learning on the job. So, when I encourage you to seek out challenges on the job, I trust that you find this to be a welcome proposition.

GUIDANCE FOR ORGANIZATIONS

CHAPTER 26
RETURN ON IMPROVED PERFORMANCE

"HOW CONCERNED WOULD you be if your HR strategy fell into the competition's hands? If your answer is 'not very,' can your organization be making world-class decisions where talent matters most to your strategic success?"

—John Boudreau and Peter Ramstad, *Beyond HR: The New Science of Human Capital*

This chapter and the one that follows it are for people involved in developing leadership across an organization. This includes HR leaders, learning and development professionals, and people leading talent strategies. It also includes executives who take leadership development seriously and view it as part of their day-to-day responsibilities. Although these suggestions will be most helpful for people working in large organizations, I expect them to be relevant to growing startups that understand how growing leadership talent can boost their success.

A recent study of line managers and HR leaders asked people to state to what extent they agree with the following statement:

> Business leaders' decisions that depend upon or affect human capital (e.g. layoffs, rewards, etc.) are as rigorous, logical, and strategically relevant as their decisions about resources such as money, technology, and customers.

Possible answers ranged from 1 ("to little or no extent") to 5 ("to a very great extent"). The average score by line managers was 3.2. The average score by HR leaders was 2.9.

In short, both groups saw significant room for improvement in the rigor and logic that go into making decisions about talent.[74] This has a big implication for HR leaders, learning and development professionals, and managers committed to developing talent. It means that it's not enough to understand your organization's strategy and provide programs and resources that support this strategy. Nor is it enough to be a savvy business partner or "have a seat at the table." These are necessary but not sufficient to significantly influence organizational performance. What's called for is a more rigorous method of *making decisions* involving talent.

John Boudreau, one of the study's authors, refers to this method as a decision science. He points out that both finance and marketing are decision sciences because they provide frameworks for managers to make decisions. Finance decision frameworks include net present value and return on investment. For marketing, the list includes segmentation and product life cycles. In both cases, the availability of decision frameworks means that these functional areas (finance and marketing) influence decisions by senior leaders even when their practitioners (finance and marketing professionals) are not in the room.

Wouldn't it be nice to have a substantial influence on decisions that affect leadership development and top talent even when you aren't part of the discussion? Wouldn't it be great to have your decision frameworks do the work for you?

This may seem like a pipe dream. However, I view it as one of those unconventional ideas that, if taken seriously, has the potential to produce enormous innovation.

In *Beyond HR*, another book by Boudreau, he and his coauthor, Peter Ramstad, offer a decision framework that holds great promise for leadership development. It's the concept of Return on Improved Performance or ROIP. Boudreau and Ramstad illustrate this concept through the example of a Disney theme park. What, they ask, has a greater impact on the park's success: improving the quality of the Mickey Mouse characters or improving the quality of the street sweepers? Mickey Mouse is the star of the park, so it's him, right? Not quite. The question isn't who is the most important person, but instead whose improvement will have the biggest impact. Most Mickey Mouse characters are very entertaining. The difference between an *A Player* Mickey Mouse and a *B Player* Mickey Mouse isn't obvious to most park visitors. In contrast, improving the quality of a street sweeper can have a large impact on visitors' enjoyment. A *B Player* street sweeper does a nice job sweeping and acts politely toward visitors. An *A Player* street sweeper does much more. He notices when you're lost and provides directions. He says something clever that surprises you way more than if you heard it from Mickey Mouse. The ROIP for the street sweeper exceeds the ROIP for Mickey Mouse.

That's why the framework is called return on improved performance, not return on performance. The key word is *improved*. How much more strategic value does the organization get when you improve the performance of a particular position like street sweeper? Similarly, how much more strategic value does the organization get when you improve a particular skill, like giving excellent directions? Once you hear these questions, they sound obvious and logical. However, most organizations rarely ask them. As a result, organizations that do ask them have an opportunity to distinguish themselves in the marketplace.

The concept of Return on Improved Performance can improve decision-making about leadership development. In particular, it suggests that you ask the following questions in order to maximize your return on investment:

- Which leaders are most likely to maximize the learning from investments in their development? The answer, as we've seen, is leaders with high learning agility. They learn the most from their experience and therefore are most likely to improve their future performance.

- Which leaders' improved performance will have the largest strategic impact on the organization? This question is trickier to answer than the one about Disney theme parks, because leaders influence business outcomes over time and mostly indirectly through others' actions. One way to make this assessment is to explore which leaders' improved performance will have the greatest impact on the performance of the people around them. Alternatively, you can look at which people are currently managing businesses, functions, or initiatives where the organization is placing a big bet on its future.[75]

- How much will you invest in each leader? Many organizations take a one-size-fits-all approach. They give all leaders the same amount of coaching, training, or mentoring. Or they allocate equal time in talent development discussions to all of their high potential talent. This seems fair, but it's not necessarily smart or logical. Remember Disney. Street sweepers have a higher ROIP than Mickey Mouse. What's the equivalent in leadership? Start by exploring how much strategic impact each leader's improved performance will have on the organization. Whose improved performance will have the largest impact on people around them? Who currently manages businesses or functions where the organization is placing a big bet on its future or where the largest number of dollars are involved? It may make sense to invest more leadership development resources in this person than in someone with a lower ROIP.

• For each selected leader, what skills or capabilities, if improved, will have the most significant impact on her performance?

These questions open the door to rigorous thinking and high quality strategic conversations about leadership development. They are deceptively simple. If you bring them to a team of five people responsible for leadership development, be prepared to hear five different perspectives. This is precisely the point. Making solid decisions about leadership development requires rigorous and respectful debate about how to maximize return on investment. By exploring these questions, you can get a clearer picture of *who* to invest in, *how much* to invest in them, and *what* skills they will develop.

There is one more piece to the puzzle. How can you help these pivotal leaders develop critical skills in a way that maximizes their learning? Better yet, what portfolio of investments in leadership development will generate the largest improvement in leadership skills and capabilities?

These are large questions without simple answers. I bring them up as an open challenge to anyone willing and able to grapple with them. For most of us, there is a simpler way to ask the *how* question. Once you've identified the specific investments your organization will make in leadership development, how can you maximize the return on these investments? This is the topic of the next chapter.

CHAPTER 27
TIPS FOR DESIGNING PROGRAMS

"FOR EVERY HOUR of competition, spend five hours practicing."
—Daniel Coyle, *The Little Book of Talent*

We are always in the middle of something. If your job involves leadership development, it's unlikely that at the very moment you are reading this book, you are creating a strategy from scratch. Instead, your plate is full of existing projects like helping a large division identify, assess, and develop its top talent. Or you are creating new programs like an action learning project that will take on tough strategic issues or an executive coaching program that will serve 150 leaders in ten countries. How can you produce the most leadership development—and improved performance—from these investments? What tips from this book will be most useful to you in making decisions in the coming weeks and months?

The answers to these questions depend on the specific activities and initiatives you are designing or managing. So let's explore a set of tips for each of the following activities: top talent selection, succession planning, executive coaching, development plans, cohort learning, action learning, formal training, and strategy execution.

TOP TALENT SELECTION

Description:

Identify the people that your organization considers its up-and-coming or high potential leaders. These are people in whom you will invest significant leadership development resources and watch closely as part of succession planning.

Tips:

- Assess people based upon both their performance and their potential.

- When you look at their potential, pay close attention to their learning agility or capacity to derive lessons from their experiences. One way to do this is through an instrument like Lominger's Learning Agility Architect. Another is to interview prospective top talent and their past managers about the challenging experiences they had and what they learned from them.

- Look broadly. Don't just consider the "golden boys," the people (often male) who speak up the most, or the ones who've had the biggest successes. Spend time with introverts, promising female leaders, and people who've taken professional risks and made the best of difficult situations.

- If you are a senior executive, get personally involved in making these assessments. If you are in HR, executive development, or learning and development, focus on ensuring a quality process that focuses on relevant questions.

Succession Planning

Description:

Create a robust and flexible system for developing the leadership capabilities of top talent and preparing them for senior executive roles.

Tips:

- Integrate succession planning with leadership development. Every time you have a conversation about succession, ask: how might this be a developmental opportunity? Every time you have a conversation about leadership development, ask: what roles are we preparing this person for, and what challenging experiences can help prepare them?

- Identify the positions that teach people the lessons they need to learn to guide the organization's strategy over the next five years. What curriculum does each position provide?

- When hiring people for these linchpin roles, base the hiring decision not only on who is most likely to succeed in the job, but also on who can learn the most from the experience.

- When weighing the risk of hiring someone who is not the perfect fit but could get the most from the experience, consider how much of this risk can be absorbed by the people who will be around them. Will their new boss, peers, and direct reports be highly competent at their respective roles? If so, then hiring someone with only 80 percent of what they need to succeed is less of a risk to the overall system.

- In the words of Jeannie Coyle, don't play dominoes or checkers. Play chess.[76] Dominoes involves asking: if one falls, who's next in line? Checkers involves asking a somewhat more complex question: who's ready to move, and where should they move next? Chess involves in-depth thinking and conversation about both people and positions. It includes thinking several moves ahead, looking at multiple scenarios, and discussing tradeoffs in potential moves.

EXECUTIVE COACHING

Description:

Support leaders in realizing their full potential and preparing for more senior roles through a relationship with a skilled executive coach.

Tips:

- Make executive coaching available primarily to leaders who have both performed well and demonstrated an ability to learn from their experiences.

- When holding initial conversations with leaders thinking about getting coached, listen for experiences that have ignited their commitment to improve. Ask them to tell you what these moments meant to them.

- Offer coaching rather than requiring it. Grant leaders the freedom as adults to decide whether or not they want to invest their time in coaching. Remember: the more open people are to developing themselves, the more they will get out of the experience.

- Watch for situations in which a coachee's direct manager suggests that he get coached because the manager isn't comfortable giving him direct feedback. At a minimum, insist that the direct manager get involved in coaching by providing feedback and agreeing to support the outcomes of coaching. If possible, use the coaching engagement as a forum for gently teaching the direct manager how to give effective feedback.

- Hire executive coaches who understand that deliberate practice is an essential part of leadership development. It's not necessary that they use the particular practices in this book. However, think carefully before hiring a coach who doesn't incorporate deliberate practice into the services they provide.

- Create practice fields where small groups of leaders currently receiving coaching (from the same coach or different coaches) can go to directly practice key skills. When possible, bring together people who are practicing similar skills (like asking powerful questions or turning toward others) so they can practice the same thing at the same time.

- Create a menu of coaching services leaders can select from, based on the perceived value and their budgets. On this menu, include the following: shadowing the leader during live meetings and providing him with immediate feedback, building a feedback system around the leader by teaching stakeholders how to give direct and specific feedback, and extended practice sessions.

- When bringing together executive coaches who support your organization's leaders, ask them to talk in detail about how they help their clients practice both directly and on the job. This will allow them to learn from each other and therefore better serve your organization's leaders.

- Apply this list of tips to internal coaches, people employed by your organization who provide coaching to others in the organization.

DEVELOPMENT PLANS

Description:

Create and commit to written plans to guide a leader's development over the next year.

Tips:

- Ensure that every development plan identifies challenging experiences—in the current role or a new role—that will teach the lessons the person needs to learn to guide the company in five years.

- Include specific ways that the person will maximize what she learns from these experiences through on-the-job-practice. How will she build preparation and reflection into her calendar? What feedback will she request from which people?

- Focus the development plan on at least one inner and one outer practice of leadership development. Use this book and others as sources for these practices. What matters most is that they be actionable and practicable.

- Differentiate between (a) hard, high-precision skills like staying calm during heated discussions by following a prescribed sequence of steps and (b) soft, high-flexibility skills like artfully blending with another person's opinions.

- Identify specifically where and how the leader will practice each skill.

- Include support structures that will accelerate her learning. These include exemplars of the skill she can observe, development

partners practicing similar skills, and trusted colleagues with
whom to safely share learning.

- Provide checkpoint dates for the leader to talk with her manager
  about progress and challenges.

COHORT LEARNING

Description:

A group of leaders (often high-potentials from different parts of an
organization) who meet regularly as a group over six months or more in a
safe space for learning, reflection, and practice.

Tips:

- When selecting participants, pick leaders who are skilled at
  learning from experience.

- Incorporate the on-the-job-practice cycle by giving people time
  to prepare for upcoming on-the-job experiences and reflect upon
  experiences they have had.

- Give participants an opportunity to directly practice skills that are
  specific to their development. Don't expect everyone to practice
  the same things. Ensure that participants have a chance to stretch
  themselves and get live feedback. Whenever possible, match up
  people practicing similar skills.

- Provide time for participants to discuss ways to get more value
  from their existing day-to-day support systems. How can they get
  better feedback from the people around them? What are more
  effective ways of managing their calendars? What people and
  commitments are helping them increase their physical energy?

- Encourage participants to find a buddy in the class and commit to a series of regular check-in conversations focused on specific topics and questions.

ACTION LEARNING

Description:

A diverse group of high potential leaders takes on a temporary assignment to jointly explore a thorny business issue. The result is a recommendation to top executives. During the process, participants practice new behaviors, reflect, and get feedback from a coach.

Tips:

- When selecting participants, pick leaders who are skilled at learning from experience.

- Ask participants to identify up front one or two actionable leadership skills they will practice. Invite them to share these development areas with other participants to build trust and initiate feedback systems.

- Integrate the on-the-job-practice cycle into the team calendar. Include time for preparation, reflection, and feedback.

- Provide short teaching modules in chunks. For example, right before a heated discussion, spend 45 minutes talking about how to argue better, ask powerful questions, or listen like a master.

- Insert brief reflection moments into the middle of team meetings. Challenge people to pause, reflect on their behaviors, and consider ways to improve their performance.

- Provide on-on-one coaching to participants to help them achieve their unique learning outcomes and get the most value from the action learning experience. When possible, expand this coaching to also focus on participants' regular jobs.

- Ask participants' direct managers to support their development to whatever degree the managers are willing.

- Give participants' teams and regular working colleagues an opportunity to "send them off" to action learning with a specific challenge and, later, to "receive" them and publicly acknowledge their learning.

FORMAL TRAINING

Description:

Classes held outside the flow of day-to-day work and focused on building skills.

Tips:

- Build formal training around existing work commitments and arrangements. Provide training to intact teams, temporary working groups, task forces, and people engaging in strategic initiatives. Give people the opportunity to prepare for, reflect on, and get feedback about their experiences from the people they work with.

- Provide the training in short chunks and schedule it around existing work commitments. For example, if an executive team is about to hold a two-day strategic conversation, give them a short training in arguing better or seeing patterns right before starting that conversation.

- Focus the training not on what leaders generically need to learn, but on the specific development areas of participants. Because ten people may have ten different development areas, design in ways for each participant to develop the skills that matter to her.

- Include time for participants to directly practice skills. Challenge them with games and other methods of stretching their capabilities.

- Involve executives and managers as teachers. Tap people who model excellence in a particular skill. Give them a chance to demonstrate it and talk about it.

- When designing a class, start by assuming that one hundred percent of it will involve deliberate practice rather than trying to find ways to squeeze deliberate practice into a conventional training format.

STRATEGY EXECUTION

Description:

An organization-wide effort to transform what it does, who it serves, and how it operates. The measure of success is that people at every level of the organization are practicing new behaviors that align with the new strategy.

Tips:

- As described in the chapter on seeing patterns, invest executive attention in recognizing emergent strategies. These are patterns of past behavior within an organization that signal a new direction. Support the best of these strategies by codifying them as deliberate strategies. This is how many of the best strategies form.

This also eliminates the need to convince everyone to act in new ways; many of them are already doing so.

- Challenge and support all senior executives to improve their skill at telling powerful stories.

- After declaring a new strategy, convene a multitude of conversations for possibility in which people imagine what life might look like in this new future. Improve people's performance in these conversations by giving them just-in-time learning chunks about conversations for possibility, asking powerful questions, and listening like a master. Whenever possible, directly involve senior executives in these conversations (by asking questions, describing scenarios, and listening) rather than relying entirely on facilitators.

- Before asking people to take on new behaviors, identify the new core promises that the organization will be making to customers. Who will be promising what to whom by when? After getting clear on these new core promises, determine what networks of promises need to be built within the organization to deliver on these core promises to customers. Who will be promising what to whom by when?

- After identifying the network of promises, challenge each person involved in delivering on a promise to assess their competence— and their team's competence—to successfully fulfill it. Use these assessments to identify the key skills that particular people and teams need to develop. Build all subsequent learning and practice around these skills.

- Strategy execution involves selecting people for both permanent and temporary roles. When making these decisions, draw upon the tips for succession planning, like hiring people for their learning agility in addition to their past performance.

•   Remember the pivotal role that physical energy plays in performance. When asking people to bring about a new strategy, provide structured support for them to increase their physical energy. Be willing to dramatically change how the organization works with calendars. Recognize that people need a short break every 90 minutes. Make it OK to take short naps. Ensure that the company cafeteria serves food that supports sustained energy rather than blood sugar spikes and crashes.

EPILOGUE
TOWARD A NEW WAY OF BEING

"THERE IS NOTHING like returning to a place that remains unchanged to find the ways in which you yourself have been altered."
—Nelson Mandela

This book started with an event that had a one in ten thousand chance of occurring. It taught me that life can change from a single improbable act. I'd like to end the book showing a second way that life can change: from long-term deliberate practice. Here are three stories that illustrate the possibility of great leadership as a permanent way of living:

Drew (a composite of two people) has been a senior manager for twenty years. He is known for accomplishing big things, staying positive, and giving polished presentations. He works hard and is proud of his feats. However, interviews reveal that most people who work with him feel like they don't really know him and wonder about his sincerity. *Is this what he really feels or is this just for show?* This assessment hits Drew hard, but after significant reflection he acknowledges that he actually doesn't know what he's feeling most of the time, so how could others? This suppression of feeling is a direct expression of his Achilles' Heel. After three months of observing his own emotions and learning the language of emotion (sadness, fear, contentment, disgust, delight, etc.), he starts to practice a new way of speaking. To be specific, he starts to practice speaking authentically, which includes revealing what he is feeling. He also begins to listen more deeply to others. Neither practice is easy— after all, he is a beginner at this emotional stuff—but over time he gets the hang of it and even starts to enjoy it.

How do others respond? At first, they're not sure what to think. *Drew sure is acting strangely.* But when they see this behavior show up more consistently, they begin to appreciate it—and trust him. *I really know where he's coming from. He feels real.* As others develop greater trust in Drew's sincerity, they sign on wholeheartedly to his big visions.

Gina (also a composite) is a bright 40-something leader in a Fortune 100 company with great potential. Her greatest asset is discernment. She can pinpoint what's missing in a plan or strategy and suggest how to improve it. She also takes care of her staff and is widely respected for her competence and integrity. Yet, like Drew, she has an Achilles' Heel. Instead of sincerity, her issue is appreciation. It is not uncommon for her to publicly criticize others' ideas and even disparage them as individuals. This is particularly true with peers, several of whom tell me she has an "attitude" and is "hard to work with because you never know what she's going to say about you." When hearing this assessment, Gina readily agrees that it sounds like her. On a deeper level, we discover that the voice inside her head that can be critical of others is actually brutal toward herself. This "inner critic" is part pit bull, part sniper, and always on the attack.

After observing it in action for a few weeks, she takes on two new practices: keeping a list of what she is grateful for that day (a sly way of calling B.S. on her critical mind) and doing a physical movement that makes her body more flexible (and improves her posturing). Over time, these practices quiet her inner critic and help her accept others' flaws and mistakes. She "neutral"izes two key relationships that were on the rocks and builds a more positive public identity in the company.

In 1997 *Shawn Green* (his real name, but not someone I've coached) was a talented Major League Baseball player who was frustrated by being benched. Not only that, but after a confrontation with the team's batting coach, he was prohibited from going to the batting cage without the coach's supervision—an insulting restriction. Rather than sulk in resentment and resignation, Shawn started a new practice. He found a batting tee and net in a little-used area outside the clubhouse and started hitting by himself. (Batting tees are decidedly *not* how pros practice.) He visualized game situations and pretended that "I was facing all of the pitchers I was currently being forced to watch from the dugout...[and] notice[d] the sound of the ball swishing against the back net." His mind quieted and his breathing became "rhythmic." He repeated this batting meditation every day.

In his first at bat after being placed in the lineup, he hit a home run against the All-Star pitcher, Greg Maddux. Within a month, his batting average had increased by sixty points. At first teammates teased him about traveling with a tee, but over time they gained respect for this unorthodox practice. In the coming years, he added other deliberate practices like improving his stride by "imagining with my foot and shoulder" and anticipating pitches by carefully watching individual pitchers and keeping a journal of their patterns. The result? A fifteen-year career with a lifetime .280 batting average and over 300 home runs, including four homers in a single game (a record).[77]

As someone biologically wired more for negative than positive emotion, I find stories like these to be inspiring. They challenge me to live and lead with my best stuff even when the odds are stacked against me. And they remind me that just as great leadership inevitably requires an encounter with fear-based cultures, the path to great leadership winds through the valley of risk and awkwardness. This is because:

- The practices that evoke greatness are unusual and often uncomfortable—at least at first.

- These practices are also uncommon and can look "weird." Others may have negative judgments about them. So may you.

- An effective set of practices shifts your outer behaviors while simultaneously growing your inner experiences into healthier and more mature forms.

- When you select practices wisely and practice them deliberately, the results speak for themselves. Others' negative judgment morphs into respect, and your own discomfort shifts into pride that you are leading at your best.

Enjoy the practicing and drop me a line (amiel@amielhandelsman.com) to let me know how it's going.

NOTES

[1] Unfortunately, few HR leaders alive today are aware of the requirement that training content match on-the-job learning.

[2] Corporate Leadership Council. *Realizing the Full Potential of Rising Talent*, 2005.

[3] Eichinger, Robert. Slides from presentation to Human Resource Planning Society.

[4] Lominger, *The Leadership Architect Norms and Validity Report*, 2003.

[5] McCall, Morgan, M. Lombardo and A. Morrison. *The Lessons of Experience: How Successful Executives Develop on the Job*. New York, NY: Lexington Books, 1988, p. 10.

[6] Douglas, Christina. *Key Events and Lessons for Managers in a Diverse Workforce*. Greensboro, NC: Center for Creative Leadership, 2003.

[7] Hewitt Associates, *Top Companies for Leaders*, 2005.

[8] Human Resources Institute.

[9] Conger, Jay and Robert Fulmer. "Build a Better Leadership Pipeline." Center for Effective Organizations, January 2004.

[10] Conaty, Bill and Ram Charan. *The Talent Masters: Why Smart Leaders Put People Before Numbers*. Crown Publishing Group, 2010, p. 97.

[11] Coyle, Jeannie and Wendy Axelrod. *Make Talent Your Business: How Exceptional Managers Develop People While Getting Results*. New York, NY: Berrett-Koehler, 2011.

[12] Coyle, Jeannie and Wendy Axelrod. *Make Talent Your Business*.

[13] Jim and John Harbaugh, who coached against each other in the 2013 Super Bowl, both send game film each week to their father, Jack Harbaugh, a former college coach. Every Tuesday, Jack watches both films in case either son calls to get his perspective. Source: *The Herd with Colin Cowherd*. ESPN Radio, June 14, 2013.

[14] Colvin, Geoff. *Talent Is Overrated: What Really Separates World-Class Performers From Everybody Else.* New York, NY: Portfolio Trade, 2010.

[15] Coyle, Daniel. *The Talent Code: Greatness Isn't Born. It's Grown. Here's How.* New York, NY: Bantam, 2009.

[16] Gladwell, Malcolm. *Outliers: The Story of Success.* New York, NY: Little Brown & Company, 2008.

[17] See for example Gallup's 2012 study *Engagement at Work: Its Effect on Performance Continues in Tough Economic Times.* Available on www.gallup.com

[18] Rock, David. "Managing with the Brain in Mind." *Strategy + Business*, Autumn 2009.

[19] Boudreau, John W. "Retooling HR: Using Proven Business Tools to Make Better Decisions About Talent." *Harvard Business Review Press*, 2010, Kindle locations 437–440.

[20] Eichenwald, Kurt. "Microsoft's Lost Decade." *Vanity Fair*, August 2012.

[21] When Adobe ended its performance review system, it saved 80,000 hours of work per year.

[22] One piece of good news: Microsoft ended its forced ranking system late in 2013.

[23] Coyle, Daniel. *The Little Book of Talent.* New York, NY: Bantam, 2012.

[24] Collins, Jim. *Good to Great.* New York, NY: HarperBusiness, 2001, pp. 37–38.

[25] Some have cited Gilligan's *In A Different Voice* as evidence that women, unlike men, are not hierarchical. However, her research suggests that although women are more likely than men to *think* non-hierarchically, they *develop* through successive hierarchical stages, each more inclusive than the prior one.

[26] Grove, Andrew. *Only the Paranoid Survive: How to Exploit the Crisis Points That Challenge Every Company.* New York, NY: Currency, 1996, pp. 89–90.

[27] For the full story, you'll have to wait for my next book, tentatively titled *The Purple Couch and Other Leadership Lessons from a Decade of Dating*.

[28] Gottman, John M. *The Relationship Cure: A 5 Step Guide to Strengthening Your Marriage, Family and Friendships*. New York, NY: Three Rivers Press, 2001.

[29] This is not a typo. Gottman's research shows that the fastest way to end a relationship is to turn *away from* the other person's bids.

[30] Quoted in Dahle, Cheryl. "What Are You Complaining About?" *Fast Company*, May 2001.

[31] I am taking the liberty to use Gottman's phrases in the context of responding to complaints. These applications are mine, not his.

[32] Kegan, Robert and L. Lahey. *How the Way We Talk Can Change the Way We Work: Seven Languages for Transformation*. San Francisco: Jossey-Bass, 2002.

[33] Marshall, Lisa. *Speak the Truth and Point to Hope: The Leader's Journey to Maturity*. Dubuque, Iowa: Kendall/Hunt, 2004.

[34] "A Conversation on Leadership with Carol and Jack Weber." *Virginia Business*, July 2007.

[35] Founder of New Ventures West. See his book *Coaching: Evoking Excellence in Others*. Boston: Butterworth Heinemann, 1999.

[36] Brownell, Judi. *Fostering Service Excellence Through Listening*. The Center for Hospitality Research, Cornell University, 2009.

[37] I have adapted this list of listening filters from a model of personal development called the Enneagram.

[38] Mintzberg, Henry, B. Ahlstrand and J. Lampel. *Strategy Bites Back: It Is Far More and Less Than You Ever Imagined*. Upper Saddle River, NJ: Pearson Prentice Hall, 2005.

[39] For a summary of the original BCG case and Pascale's findings, see Mintzberg, Henry, B. Ahlstrand and J. Lampel. *Strategy Safari: A Guided Tour Through the Wilds of Strategic Management*. New York, NY: Free Press, 1998.

[40] Siegel, Daniel. *Mindsight: The New Science of Personal Transformation*. New York, NY: Bantam Books, 2011.

[41] McCall, Morgan. "The Experience Conundrum." *Harvard Business Press Chapters,* 2010.

[42] Riso, Don R. and R. Hudson. *Personality Types: Using the Enneagram for Self-Discovery.* Boston: Houghton Mifflin, 1996.

[43] www.hoganassessments.com

[44] Hogan, Joyce, R. Hogan and R. Kaiser. *Management Derailment: Personality Assessment and Mitigation.* Downloaded from www.hoganassessments.com

[45] Seligman, Martin. *Authentic Happiness. Using the New Positive Psychology to Realize Your Potential for Lasting Fulfillment.* New York, NY: Atria, 2003.

[46] Argyris, Chris. *Overcoming Organizational Defenses.* New York, NY: Prentice Hall, 1990.

[47] Michael now runs his own company, Truly Productive.

[48] Allen, David. *Getting Things Done: The Art of Stress-Free Productivity.* New York, NY: Penguin, 2002.

[49] Remind me to include this on the list of powerful questions in the next edition of this book.

[50] Mintzberg, Henry. *Managing.* New York, NY: Berrett-Koehler, 2009.

[51] Quoted in Tony Schwartz's book *Be Excellent at Anything.*

[52] You can read about rebound exercise on Wikipedia. See http://en.wikipedia.org/wiki/Rebound_exercise. You can find out more about Jordan's SuperBound® approach at ReboundWorld.com.

[53] I first encountered this concept in Shawn Phillips's *Strength for Life.*

[54] Buettner, Dan. *Blue Zones: Lessons for Living Longer from the People Who've Lived the Longest.* Washington DC: National Geographic, 2010.

[55] Schwartz, Tony. *Be Excellent at Anything: The Four Keys to Transforming the Way We Work and Live.* New York, NY: Free Press, 2010.

[56] Schwartz, Tony. *Be Excellent At Anything.*

[57] www.seanleclaire.com

[58] Coyle, Daniel. *The Little Book of Talent.* New York, NY: Bantam, 2012.

[59] Coyle, Daniel. *The Little Book of Talent,* pp. 7–8.

[60] Coyle, Daniel. *The Little Book of Talent*, pp. 15–16.

[61] Coyle, Daniel. *The Little Book of Talent*, pp. 17–20.

[62] Coyle, Daniel. *The Little Book of Talent*, pp. 41–43.

[63] Coyle, Daniel. *The Little Book of Talent*, p. 44.

[64] Coyle, Daniel. *The Little Book of Talent*, pp. 62–63.

[65] Coyle, Daniel. *The Little Book of Talent*, pp. 97–98.

[66] Coyle, Daniel. *The Little Book of Talent*, pp. 101–103.

[67] Coyle, Daniel. *The Little Book of Talent*, pp. 110–111.

[68] Quoted in Mintzberg's book *Managing*. The original study appeared in Mintzberg's first book, *The Nature of Managerial Work*, 1973.

[69] Mintzberg, Henry. *Managing*.

[70] Torbert, William. *Action Inquiry: The Secret of Timely and Transforming Leadership*. San Francisco: Berrett-Koehler, 2004.

[71] The Five Whys is part of the Toyota Production System or "lean" management. For applications of lean, look at Mark Graban's blog (www.leanblog.org). For a strategic perspective, check out *The Hitchhiker's Guide to Lean* by Jamie Flinchbaugh and Andy Carlino.

[72] Joiner, Bill and S. Josephs. *Leadership Agility: Five Levels of Mastery for Anticipating and Initiating Change*. San Francisco: Wiley, 2007.

[73] Charan, Ram and B. Conaty. *The Talent Masters: Why Smart Leaders Put People Before Numbers*. New York, NY: Random House, 2011.

[74] Lawler, Ed and John Boudreau. *Achieving Excellence in Human Resources Management*. Palo Alto, CA: Stanford Business Books, 2009.

[75] *Beyond HR* provides a back-of-the-envelope approach to comparing the ROIPs of different people and different skills. Drawing simple graphs allows you to bring greater rigor to such decisions. It is an alternative both to ignoring the question and to complicating it by trying to quantify it unnecessarily.

[76] Coyle, Jeannie. *Strategic HR Consulting, Applied to Talent Review*. Report for corporate client.

[77] Greene, Shawn. *The Way of Baseball: Finding Stillness at 95 MPH*. New York, NY: Simon & Schuster, 2011.

ACKNOWLEDGEMENTS

I am deeply grateful to the many managers who have invited me into their lives as their coach, whether for three months or three years. It is an incredible honor.

This is my first book, so I thank several other *firsts*:

- Frank H., the first person I coached; Doug S., the first person I coached for an extended period of time; Kathy Burke, the first person who coached me; and Pam Weiss, Sarita Chawla, and James Flaherty, my first and best coaching teachers.

- Mike Cohen, my first true adult best friend; Jon Rubenstein and Michael Dolan for being first to JAM; Simon Turkalj for being the first person I turn to for creative provocation; Steve March for first showing me what a real book collection looks like; Bill Hefferman for first modeling how to use a strengths-based approach in a big company; Janet Crawford for first showing me the connection between brain science and leadership; and Raleigh Woods for first teaching me how to argue about sports and politics with gusto and humor.

As I think about the professional opportunities in my life, I feel gratitude for the following people:

- Ed O'Neil and Rob Williams, who took a chance on a 22-year-old and launched a career.
- Stacy Flaherty, who brought me into the center of New Ventures West's wonderful community.

- Rob Pasick, Donna Fowler, Dana Brenner-Kelly, Julie Rubinstein, Cy Hufano, Lori Emerick, Mariann Pike, Lynette Winter, Jennifer Wallace, Rand Schenck, Kristen Krull, Carla Blackadder, Dale Fruehauf, and John Johnson, all of who made pivotal connections that allowed me to serve more leaders.
- Cindy Becker, who trusted me to help transform a public sector organization from the inside.
- Jeannie Coyle, who re-introduced me to the CCL research, and Jan Carothers of NSA Oregon, who encouraged me to write.

My intellectual forebears are tall and numerous:

- Ken Wilber, Bill Torbert, Robert Kegan, Lisa Lahey, Susanne Cook-Greuter, Bill Joiner, Stephen Josephs, Sean Hargens, Jennifer Garvey-Berger, and others who have advanced integral and constructivist adult developmental theory.
- Russ Hudson and Don Riso, whose approach to the Enneagram pervades everything I do.
- James Flaherty for giving me a learning curriculum that will keep me busy for the next few decades.
- Fernando Flores, Chauncey Bell, Matthew Budd, Tracy Goss, Alan Sieler, and other practitioners of speech acts, language, and conversations.
- Martin Seligman, Marcus Buckingham, Donald Clifton, John Gottman, Tom Rath, Mihaly Csikszentmaihalyi, Sonya Lyubomirsky, Robert Quinn, Jane Dutton, and other thought leaders in positive psychology and the strengths-based school of leadership development.
- Daniel Coyle, Geoff Colvin, and Malcolm Gladwell for their inspiring books about the pivotal role of practice in high performance.
- Henry Mintzberg for offering a dynamic and integrative understanding of strategy.

- Art Kleiner, whose books about corporate heretics and core groups remind me of what's possible and why it's so hard.
- Tony Schwartz, Shawn Phillips, Jerzy and Aniela Gregorek, Jonny Bowden, Christine Caldwell, Rob Wolf, and Tim Ferriss for influencing my understanding of health, nutrition, sleep, and physical energy.

I thank Elizabeth Fausnight for skilled copy editing and Shoshana Rosenfeld for sound advice on branding.

Oh… did I mention I have an amazing family?

- My four wonderful parents, who have each contributed something special to my life, Larry and Joanne Handelsman and Wendy and Phil Baia.
- My brother, Alex, who introduced me to the Paleo diet and challenged me to write a book *now*.
- My sister, Valerie, for the guidance about mud masks and living life with zest.
- My aunt, Linda Handelsman, for introducing me to the virtues of dark chocolate.
- My sister- and brother-in-law, Wendy Endress and Bill Livingston, who have hosted me countless times on business trips up to Tacoma and Seattle.
- My sons, Jacob and Zander, who never cease to delight and intrigue me.

Last but not least, thank you, Julie, for supporting this project—and me—with love and patience.

Made in the USA
San Bernardino, CA
27 May 2014